Voices from Hudson Bay
Cree Stories from York Factory

In *Voices from Hudson Bay* Cree elders recall the daily lives and experiences of the men and women who lived and worked at the Hudson's Bay Company post at York Factory in Manitoba. Their stories, their memories of family, community, and daily life, define their past and provide insights into a way of life that has largely disappeared in northern Canada.

The era the elders describe, from the end of World War I to the closing of York Factory in 1957, saw dramatic changes to aboriginal life in the North. The extension of Treaty Five in 1910 to include members of the York Factory band, the arrival of police and government agents, and the shifting economy of the fur trade are all discussed. The elders' accounts demonstrate the continuity, despite these upheavals, of northern life in the twentieth century, from the persistence of traditional ways to the ongoing role of community and kinship ties.

Perceptions of aboriginal life have been shaped largely by non-Native accounts that offer limited views of Swampy Cree history and record little beyond the social and economic interaction that was part of life in the fur trade. The stories in this collection provide Cree perspectives on northern life and history, and represent the legacy of a younger generation of aboriginal people.

FLORA BEARDY is a historic site interpreter with Parks Canada.
ROBERT COUTTS is a historian with Parks Canada.

Voices from Hudson Bay

Cree Stories from York Factory

COMPILED AND EDITED BY

FLORA BEARDY

AND

ROBERT COUTTS

McGill-Queen's University Press

Montreal & Kingston • London • Buffalo

© McGill-Queen's University Press 1996
ISBN 0-7735-1440-6 (cloth)
ISBN 0-7735-1441-4 (paper)

Legal deposit fourth quarter 1996
Bibliothèque nationale du Québec

Printed in Canada on acid-free paper
Reprinted 1997

This book has been published with the help
of a grant from Parks Canada,
Department of Canadian Heritage.

McGill-Queen's University Press is grateful to
the Canada Council for support of its
publishing program.

Canadian Cataloguing in Publication Data

Main entry under title:
Voices from Hudson Bay:
Cree stories from York Factory
(Rupert's Land Record Society series,
ISSN 1181-7461; 5)
Includes bibliographical references and index.
ISBN 0-7735-1440-6 (bound).
ISBN 0-7735-1441-4 (pbk.)
1. Cree Indians – Manitoba – York Factory –
Social life and customs – Anecdotes.
2. Cree Indians – Manitoba – York Factory –
Social conditions – Anecdotes.
3. York Factory (Man.) – Social life and customs
– Anecdotes.   4. York Factory (Man.) – Social
conditions – Anecdotes.   5. Hudson's Bay
Company – History – Anecdotes.
I. Beardy, Flora, 1946–
II. Coutts, Robert, 1953–   III. Series.
E99.C88V64 1996   971.27'1   C96-990009-0

This book was typeset by
Typo Litho Composition Inc.
in 10/13 Palatino.

Contents

Contents

Illustrations

Acknowledgments

The origins of this book go back to the spring of 1989 when, with much laughter and apprehension, we practised interviewing each other on a new tape recorder in a hotel room in Churchill, Manitoba. The many hours spent recording and transcribing the stories of Cree elders from York Factory were followed by a painstaking selection and editing process that resulted in the recollections contained in this book.

Many people provided assistance throughout the project. First, of course, we owe a great debt of gratitude to the elders who generously contributed their stories and teachings. The spirit and enthusiasm of Mr Archelaus Beardy, Mr Alex Ouscan, Mr Fred Beardy, Mr Richard Beardy, Mr and Mrs Joseph and Amelia Saunders, Mr and Mrs Albert and Amy Hill, Mr John Neepin, Mrs Elizabeth Oman, Mr David Massan, Mrs Mary Redhead, Mrs Catherine Anderson, and Mr Abel Chapman was both compelling and rewarding. Much was learned from them and we hope this publication is deserving of their trust.

The support of the chiefs and councils of the York Factory, Split Lake, Shamattawa, and Fox Lake First Nations was critical to the project's success. We would also like to thank Parks Canada, which sponsored the *Voices* oral history project and contributed financially to the publication of this book. Parks staff in Churchill provided their ideas and support, especially the late Lily McAuley, a dear friend and mentor, while Winnipeg colleagues Gary Adams and Margaret Burnip supplied advice and expertise during the initial phases of the project. Jennifer S. H. Brown, the Editor of the Rupert's Land Record Society, gave encouragement and guidance as well as her considerable editorial skills. Raymond Beaumont and the anonymous readers who reviewed the manuscript at an early stage made a number of useful suggestions, and David Pentland contributed advice regarding the many Cree words contained in the book. We would also like to thank John Buckner for his marvellous sketches that appear alongside the biographies, and Susan Plenert who drafted the maps. Jane Graham smoothed out much of the rough prose of the Introduction and notes, and Joan McGilvray of McGill-Queen's University Press helped guide us through the wonderful mysteries of publishing. Permission to quote from documents contained in the Hudson's Bay Company Archives, Provincial Archives of Manitoba, and the National Archives of Canada, is gratefully acknowledged, as is permission from these institutions to reproduce a number of the photographs which appear in the book. We would also like to thank various individuals for allowing us to publish photographs from their private collections, including John Ingram, the Flora Beardy family, and a number of the elders who were interviewed for this project. Copies of the Ingram photographs are on file with Parks Canada in Winnipeg.

Lastly, we would like to thank our families: Flora Beardy's husband Edwin and daughter Evelyn, and Robert Coutts's wife Catherine. Their encouragement and patience are appreciated beyond words.

Preface

Volumes of documentation exist on the activities of the Hudson's Bay Company at York Factory. Less is known, however, about the Cree people who once lived and worked at this great fur-trade post, known locally as *Kihci-wâskâhikan* or Great House. The York Factory Oral History Project was sponsored by Parks Canada to document Cree recollections of daily life and activities at the post in the first half of the twentieth century.

I started work on the project in 1989. It was hoped that Cree elders who had lived at York Factory, and still resided in various northern Manitoba communities, would provide us with information about their past. Since most of these individuals lived on different reserves, we contacted the chiefs and councils of various First Nations to explain the project and ask for their comments. Their response was encouraging: "If the elders agree to share their stories then the Chiefs wholly support the project." I also asked the chiefs to provide names of all the elders in each community who either had been born at York Factory or had resided there for some time. The people I interviewed were chosen from this list.

Prior to each interview I visited the elders at home in their respective communities. I introduced myself and related how I had lived at York Factory when I was a child. Their eyes lit up in recognition when I mentioned my parents' names, Alex and Eliza Spence. After spending some time getting reacquainted, I explained the project to them and asked them how they felt about making available to other people, on tape and in print, the experiences and memories of their lives at York Factory. Was it important to them that future generations, both aboriginal and non-aboriginal, have knowledge of their past? Their response was unequivocal. Without hesitation they were willing and eager to share their knowledge and stories. Some said this should have been done a long time ago while there were more elders alive to share their experiences.

Between May 1989 and September 1992, I recorded twelve interviews in the Cree language which I then translated and transcribed into English. The information gathered from these interviews will be useful, not only to Parks Canada's programs in northern Manitoba, but to Native study groups, students, and all those who have an interest in the history of subarctic communities. By agreement with the interviewees, their recordings will be deposited in the Provincial Archives of Manitoba, while copies will go to the elders or their children, and to various First Nations.

I consider myself very fortunate to have been part of this project. My contact with the elders has been personally rewarding and I am thankful to them for bringing alive the stories and traditions in our culture that I had forgotten. I encourage future generations to respect their elders and to listen to them, for they have great knowledge to pass on to us. They are our teachers.

My heartfelt thanks go out to all who shared their knowledge with me, for the wonderful support of their families, and also for the support of the chiefs and councils of the First Nations involved. The project was a great success.

With great respect this book is dedicated to all the elders, our teachers. *Êkosi.*

Flora Beardy
Churchill, Manitoba

Introduction

For most human societies storytelling has been the means by which individuals and groups have communicated their perceptions of the world around them. Oral tradition is as old as history itself and, like the written word, is a form of expression with layers of meaning and intent. From ancient stories passed down through the generations – usually referred to as "myth" – to descriptions of daily life and subsistence strategies, oral narratives represent a continuity between past and present. The spoken traditions of the Swampy Cree of the York Factory region are a window through which we can observe community memories that often transcend written history.

The York Factory Oral History Project was developed to collect and preserve these memories by recording the stories and experiences of a number of Cree elders who once lived and worked at York Factory and resided at the time of the interviews in Split Lake, Gillam, Churchill, Bird, Thompson, and York Landing. Although archival repositories contain a massive amount of written documentation, from almost exclusively non-Native sources, on the history of the aboriginal peoples who were associated with York for almost three centuries, far less material is available from the perspective of Native people themselves. Hudson's Bay Company post journals, correspondence, and account books, along with missionary and government records, provide a detailed and systematic picture of Cree peoples of the region from the perspective of Euro-Canadian observers. These accounts have largely shaped our perceptions of aboriginal life in the region and have

commonly been treated as authoritative. Yet these texts, restricted as they are by the biases of outsiders, observers, and non-
participants, offer limited views of Cree life and history and often
record little beyond the social and economic interactions that
were part of fur-trade life in the central subarctic during the centuries after contact. Although much may be learned from the
written record, for it is an invaluable ethnographic source, it is
narrated life histories that can put the meat on the bones of cultural experience. Embedded in the autobiographical themes of
daily life and religious and mythological narrative are descriptions of community experiences which reflect reconstructions of
the past that are both personal and dynamic. As oral historian
Julie Cruikshank observes, there is often little in Native oral
accounts that conforms to strict notions of Western narrative
biography. Instead, she argues, it is the "emphasis on landscape,
mythology, everyday events and the continuity between generations" which forms the core of these stories.[1] For the Cree people
of York Factory their life stories, the shared memories of family,
community, and daily life, define their past. Their telling enlarges
our understanding of what constitutes historical truth.

Over the last three decades much has been written about aboriginal life in northern Manitoba, largely focusing on Native in-
volvement in the fur trade before 1900. More recently, scholarly
interest in the early relations between Natives and newcomers,
and in the participation of aboriginal peoples in the European fur
trade during the eighteenth and nineteenth centuries, has been
broadened to encompass the study of social, economic, and
cultural themes associated with Native life in the north before
World War II. The goal of *Voices from Hudson Bay* is to expand on
ethnographic and economic analyses through first-person oral
accounts that provide a different perspective on the lives and attitudes of the York Factory Cree in the first half of the twentieth
century. Like the company journal and account book, the government census, or the missionary record, these testimonies present

---

1 Julie Cruikshank (with Angela Sidney, Kitty Smith, and Annie Ned),
   Life Lived like a Story: Life Stories of Three Yukon Native Elders (Vancouver: University of British Columbia Press 1990), 2.

complex and many-sided histories. Most important, they enlist new voices in the reconstruction of the historical past.

The written record pertaining to the history of aboriginal peoples in the York Factory district amounts to tens of thousands of pages, principally contained in the Hudson's Bay Company Archives. York Factory is one of the most extensively documented contact sites in western Canada. Its records, largely continuous from the founding of the post in the late seventeenth century to its closing in 1957, include almost 200 post journals, a number of nineteenth-century district reports, volumes of correspondence to and from the post, and roughly 2,000 account books covering the period 1688–1932. The account books offer insights into such topics as the material culture of the Cree, their seasonal movements, trade practices, provision of "country" produce, furs, and labour services, kinship patterns, and social organization, and the fluctuating animal populations within the region. For the twentieth century new types of company records, which include district reports, detailed personnel records, post manuals, a register of Native births, deaths, and marriages, and a few census records, furnish useful material for ethnohistorical study. Documents from sources other than the HBCA also exist. The journals and correspondence of the Protestant missionaries who served at York after 1850, along with the records of the Department of the Interior, Indian Affairs, the Geological Survey of Canada, and the North-West Mounted Police, contain a considerable body of information on Cree life in the region, especially after the York Factory band took treaty in 1910.[2]

---

2 For a description of the archival record pertaining to York Factory see: Victor Lytwyn, *York Factory Native Ethnohistory: A Literature Review and Assessment of Source Material*, Parks Canada, Microfiche Report Series no. 162 (Ottawa: 1984); Gary Adams, Margaret Burnip, and Robert Coutts, *York Factory Ethnohistory Project: Phase I Progress Report*, Parks Canada, Research Bulletin no. 284 (Ottawa: February 1991; and Robert Coutts, "York Factory as a Native Community: Public History Research Commemoration and the Challenge to Interpretation," *Prairie Forum* 17, no. 2 (1992): 275–94.

The oral record from York Factory is less developed. Over the years, oral accounts from the Cree of northern Manitoba have been collected by anthropologists and folklorists, but few pertain to the history of the York Factory people.[3] Narratives of aboriginal life in the Hudson Bay area written by Native people themselves largely date from the period after World War I and include traditional Swampy Cree legends compiled by the late Cree artist Jackson Beardy, and by Carl Ray and James Stevens.[4] The stories and reminiscences of Cree elders collected as part of the York Factory Oral History Project help to fill a gap by providing a first-person account of many aspects of daily life at the post, especially for the years after 1920. Although memory is often selective, these reminiscences offer a counterpoise to the written record. They represent another dimension to historical understanding, a reconstruction of the past by the people themselves.

The people of the York Factory region are usually identified in the historical and contemporary literature as belonging to a

---

3 See, for example, Robert Bell, "The History of the Che-che-puy-ew-tis: A Legend of the Northern Crees," *Journal of American Folklore* 10, no. 36 (1897); S.C. Simms, "Myths of the Bungees or Swampy Indians of Lake Winnipeg," *Journal of American Folklore* 19, no. 72 (1906); J.R. Cresswell, "Folk-Tales of the Swampy Cree of Northern Manitoba," *Journal of American Folklore* 35 (1922); J.J. Honigmann, "The Attawapiskat Swampy Cree: An Ethnographic Reconstruction," *Anthropological Papers of the University of Alaska* (Fairbanks: University of Alaska Press 1956), 23–82; and David Turner and Paul Wertman, *Shamattawa: The Structure of Social Relations in a Northern Algonkian Band*, Canadian Ethnology Service, Mercury Series Paper no. 36 (Ottawa: National Museums of Canada 1977).

4 See Maxwell Paupanekis, "The Trapper," *People and Pelts: Selected Papers of the Second North American Fur Trade Conference* (Winnipeg: Peguis Publishers 1973), 137–43; Tom Boulanger, *An Indian Remembers: My Life as a Trapper in Northern Manitoba* (Winnipeg: Peguis Publishers 1971); Jackson Beardy, "Cree Legends from Northern Manitoba" (unpublished manuscript, Dafoe Library, University of Manitoba 1971); and Carl Ray and James Stevens, *Sacred Legends of the Sandy Lake Cree* (Toronto: McClelland and Stewart 1971).

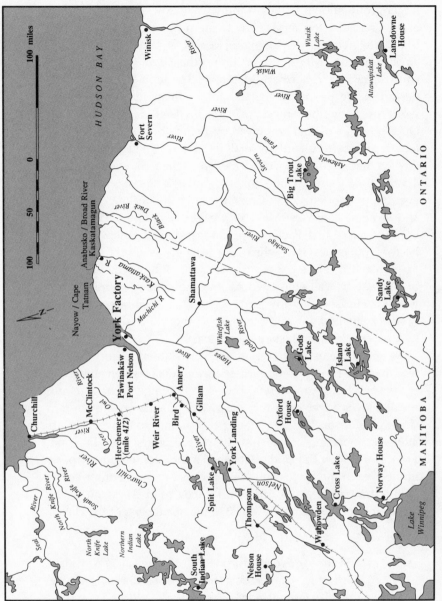

Regional setting: York Factory.

larger group known as the Swampy Cree, Lowland Cree, or West
Main Cree. The territory of the western Swampy Cree, or West
Main Cree, covers the low-lying coasts of James and Hudson
bays from the Moose River in northeastern Ontario to the
Churchill River in northern Manitoba. The term "Cree", used to
designate the people of the Canadian subarctic, comes from a
word used by the French, *Kiristinon*, itself derived from an
Ojibwa term and first employed by French traders in the seventeenth century to identify a small band that lived south of James
Bay. As these traders moved farther west, the term was applied to
a variety of groups who spoke a similar language, and it was
eventually shortened to "Cree" by English-speaking observers
and writers.[5] The West Main, or western Swampy Cree (including the Cree of York Factory) speak the n-dialect, except at Moose
Factory on James Bay where the l-dialect is used. According
to eighteenth-century HBC traders, the ethnonym *A'thinnew*
or *Athinuwick* was employed by the indigenous people of the
western Hudson Bay lowlands to identify themselves.[6] Today,
Maskêkôwininiwak [Swampy People] is the self-designation used
by Cree speakers on the bay's west coast.

As one of the oldest HBC posts in North America, York Factory
was the site of some of the earliest encounters between aboriginal
people and European traders. The post is situated near the mouth
of the Hayes River on a flat, marshy peninsula on the western
shore of Hudson Bay (see maps pp. xvii and xix). Twelve years
after the founding of the HBC in 1670, traders from England,
France, and New England established a series of temporary posts
in the area of the Hayes and Nelson rivers in hopes of attracting
Native traders from the interior. In 1684 John Abraham of the
HBC relocated his company's post to the north bank of the Hayes,

---

5 David H. Pentland, "Synonymy," in John J. Honigmann, "West Main
  Cree," *Handbook of North American Indians*, Vol. 6, *Subarctic* (Washington: Smithsonian Institution 1981), 227–8. See also Victor Lytwyn,
  "The Hudson Bay Lowland Cree in the Fur Trade to 1821: A Study in
  Historical Geography" (PHD dissertation, University of Manitoba
  1993), 28–9.
6 Lytwyn, "Hudson Bay Lowland Cree," 28.

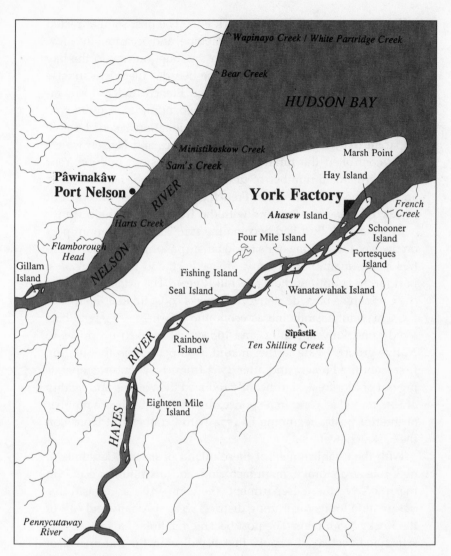

The lower Hayes and Nelson Rivers.

calling the new establishment York Fort. The post soon attracted the trade of the Cree, Ojibwa, Assiniboine, and occasionally a few other groups, who each year made the long journey to the bay from the interior. Over the next three decades there was intense competition between rival English and French traders for commercial supremacy in the region. As expanding mercantile concerns in Europe sought new areas for exploitation, it soon became apparent that whoever controlled the Hayes and Nelson waterways controlled the fur resources of the western interior. York changed hands a number of times in this period. Between 1697 and 1714 the post was under French control as Fort Bourbon, but it was ceded back to England with the Treaty of Utrecht in 1713.

By 1730 York Fort had become the HBC's most important post on the bay, the volume of its trade far surpassing that of such centres as Eastmain, Fort Albany, Moose Fort, and Prince of Wales' Fort (at the mouth of the Churchill River).[7] The establishment of the company's bayside network of posts consolidated the role of the Cree and Assiniboine as economic intermediaries who bartered guns, knives, kettles, and tobacco at marked-up prices to Native groups living farther inland. Competition in the interior, first from the French, and after 1763 from rival concerns operating out of Montreal, significantly reduced the volume and quality of furs traded at York. In response, the HBC established a number of interior posts, beginning in 1774 with Cumberland House on the Saskatchewan.

With the establishment of these inland posts, York assumed a new role as a storage, manufacturing, and distribution centre in the HBC's Northern Department, the company's administrative designation for its fur-trading districts west of Albany and east of the Rocky Mountains. The post became the hub of a vast, tightly scheduled system of supply that began with the fall arrival of the annual ships from England. Large warehouses, including the still-extant depot building, were constructed to house the many

---

7 In 1730 the volume of trade at York Factory peaked at approximately 42,000 "made beaver" (MB), compared with 8,000 MB at Prince of Wales' Fort, 11,000 MB at Albany, 4,000 MB at Moose Factory, and 3,000 MB at Eastmain. See Arthur Ray and Donald Freeman, *Give Us Good Measure* (Toronto: University of Toronto Press 1978), 34.

tons of furs, supplies, and trade goods awaiting shipment to either England or the interior. As well, York was the centre of considerable activity by artisans who manufactured a variety of articles for use in the local and inland trade. With this expanded role came new administrative and record-keeping functions, as company clerks and accountants processed the considerable volume of paperwork that accompanied the daily transactions of a major entrepôt.

By the 1850s York Factory (as it was called in the nineteenth century) had reached its peak, with over fifty buildings located at the site and a permanent workforce of some fifty-one labourers, tradespeople, clerks, and officers, many of whom were of aboriginal ancestry. Two decades later, however, the post was in decline. Changes to the HBC's transport network saw an ever-increasing volume of goods shipped to the posts of the Northwest via railways in the United States, steamboats, and Red River carts along a southern supply line headquartered at Upper Fort Garry in Red River (now Winnipeg). By 1872 York Factory was outfitting only those posts in Manitoba located north and east of Norway House, including Oxford House, Nelson House, Severn, Trout Lake, Split Lake, and Churchill. Later in the same decade the factory's accounting functions and transport responsibilities were removed to Upper Fort Garry.

In 1911 York was made the headquarters of the newly created Nelson River District, but it lost the role in 1929 to Churchill with the completion of the Hudson Bay Railway which connected Churchill with Winnipeg. York soon declined to the status of a regional trading post, and the small Cree communities at nearby Ten Shilling and French creeks were eventually abandoned in favour of settlement on the nearby Anglican mission property or on the company's 118-acre reserve at the post itself. When the factory closed in 1957 the remaining Cree families left for Split Lake, Shamattawa, and the new community at York Landing.

Throughout the transformation from trading post to entrepôt, distribution centre, and district headquarters, York Factory remained an important part of the lives of the aboriginal peoples of northern Manitoba. At the factory many assumed roles as traders, provisioners, consumers, and employees, while helping to forge a post community that possessed unique cultural characteristics as well as its own social and economic patterns and structures.

York Factory, *c.* 1853. Artist unknown. (Provincial Archives of Manitoba, Rupert's Land Collection, 13).

Even before the move inland by the HBC in 1774, a small band of coastal Cree who inhabited the area around York Factory had long specialized in supplying the post with a variety of country goods and services. The small furs, provisions, country technology, and services of the hunters, guides, packers, and couriers known as the Home-Guard Cree were indispensable to the profitability of the fur trade at York. According to Andrew Graham, who served at York for varying lengths of time between 1753 and 1772, the seasonal round of existence of the Home-Guard, both at and away from the post, was perhaps the most enduring feature of their relationship with the factory.[8] The approximately 200 men, women, and children who were then associated with York Factory pursued a variety of activities – the caribou and goose hunts and the winter trapping and summer voyaging – which were largely dictated by the seasons of the year.

Though the relatively small Home-Guard group associated with York maintained frequent contact with the factory, the post's hinterland in the coastal lowlands and the upland regions of the Hayes and Nelson rivers also included a larger population of trappers and seasonal traders. The effects of contact between the HBC traders at York Factory and these Cree people were significant and varied. Economic and social change, from alterations in material culture and patterns of resource extraction, to changes in family and kin networks, characterized life among both the York Factory Home-Guard and the upland groups who regularly traded at the post. Not the least of these effects was the devastating impact of European epidemic diseases which over three centuries took a heavy toll among the Swampy Cree of the region. Smallpox, measles, influenza, scarlet fever, and tuberculosis periodically swept through the lowlands and decimated the population. The most catastrophic of these outbreaks was the smallpox epidemic of the late eighteenth century, which first reached York from the southern plains in the spring of 1782. From company records it is estimated that during a four-year period fully one-half to two-thirds of the population of the York district

---

8 Andrew Graham, *Andrew Graham's Observations on Hudson's Bay, 1767–91*, ed. Glyndwr Williams (London: Hudson's Bay Record Society 1969), 192.

perished, a mortality rate similar to that experienced on the southern plains during the same outbreak.[9] Writing in 1786, after the epidemic had largely run its course, the chief factor at York, Humphrey Marten, described the region as "dismally depopulated."[10] In the late 1830s smallpox once more swept through the west, having spread north from the Missouri area in 1837. Although mortality rates were again high among plains tribes, the contagion had little effect on the inhabitants of the boreal forest zone and the Hudson Bay lowlands. A campaign to vaccinate western aboriginal groups, including the Home-Guard Cree of the York Factory region, had been initiated, and the proliferation of inland trading posts had relieved plains groups from having to travel as far as Hudson Bay. As a result, the outbreak of 1837–38 had little effect upon the Ojibwa, Western Woods Cree, and Swampy Cree peoples living north of the parkland zone.[11] A third smallpox epidemic, in 1869–70, again affected plains groups but had little impact on the Cree peoples of the York area.

---

9 Because of the French capture and destruction of York Factory in September 1782 records are unavailable for what was possibly the worst period of the epidemic in the Hayes-Nelson district. Estimates of mortality were made by company traders the following year when the post was re-established by the HBC. Only a handful of deaths from smallpox, however, were recorded at York itself during this period, largely because of the company's efforts to persuade Native traders to stay away from the factory. For a discussion of the effects of smallpox on the Cree of western Hudson Bay in the eighteenth century see Lytwyn, "Hudson Bay Lowland Cree," 353–73.

10 York Factory Journal, 18 June 1786, Hudson's Bay Company Archives (Winnipeg), B.239/a/86, fo. 41d.

11 Michael Payne, "Smallpox at York Factory: Epidemic Disease, Burial Practices, and the York Factory Cemetery," A Social History of York Factory, 1788–1870, Parks Canada, Microfiche Report Series no. 110 (Ottawa: 1984), 429–47. See also William B. Ewart, "Causes of Mortality in a Sub-Arctic Settlement (York Factory, Manitoba), 1714–1946," Canadian Medical Association Journal 129 (September 1983): 571–4. For a general discussion of epidemic diseases and Native populations in the west see Jody Decker, " 'We Should Never Be Again the Same People':

If smallpox posed little threat after 1784, a number of other epidemics occurred in the York area in the nineteenth and twentieth centuries. An 1819 outbreak of measles, carried by company brigades from Red River, led to many deaths. Scarlet fever, whooping cough, and influenza periodically visited the camps and settlements in the latter part of the nineteenth century. One source mentions thirty-five deaths from scarlet fever among the York Factory Cree in 1862.[12] In the twentieth century oral and written records describe widespread occurrences of scarlet fever and influenza which resulted in a high mortality in the York-Severn area in the 1920s, especially among children and the elderly.[13]

The effects of disease, combined with a depletion of fur-bearing animals in the lowlands surrounding Hudson Bay in the latter part of the eighteenth century, altered the population dynamics of the York region after 1790. While small groups of hunters and their families from the Severn River were moving into the York area, a number of Swampy Cree from the York Factory hinterland were migrating inland to the Norway House region and as far west as Cumberland House. This out-migration from York continued into the early decades of the nineteenth century and modified the population patterns that had once characterized the Hayes-Nelson district.[14]

Those Home-Guard who remained after 1821 saw their role affected by changing company policies and practices, particularly in the second half of the nineteenth century. When the HBC began to restrict its recruitment of Europeans as permanent servants for work at posts such as York Factory, it relied more heavily upon the Cree.

The Diffusion and Cumulative Impact of Acute Infectious Diseases Afflicting the Natives on the Northern Plains of the Western Interior of Canada, 1774–1839" (PHD dissertation, York University 1989).

12 As cited in Percy W. Mathews, *Notes on Diseases among the Indians Frequenting York Factory, Hudson's Bay.* (Montreal: Gazette Printing Company 1885), 13.

13 See the comments of David Massan, Fred Beardy, and Elizabeth Oman in the section entitled "Sickness and Medical Care", pp. 61–6.

14 Lytwyn, "Hudson Bay Lowland Cree," 419–28.

Traditionally hunters and provision suppliers for at least part of the year, while at other times engaging in subsistence activities outside the fur trade,[15] a number of Cree families assumed new duties at the post, primarily as wage labourers fulfilling many of the daily tasks that had once been assigned exclusively to European servants. As either part-time or permanent servants, they were engaged in a wide variety of tasks, such as voyaging on the York boats, loading and unloading goods and furs at ship time, cutting wood, packing fur, repairing and constructing inland boats and post buildings, whaling and rendering blubber, fashioning fish nets, assisting the post tradesmen, and transporting goods between storage facilities at the site. Whether permanent or part-time labourers, however, they tended to occupy the lowest levels of the hierarchy at the post in accordance with the division of work that characterized much of fur-trade mercantilism throughout the Northwest. The formation of nearby seasonal communities at French Creek and Kaskatamagun, as well as the development of a more permanent settlement at the post itself in the late nineteenth and early twentieth centuries, was indicative of York's changing composition. Once a company settlement of largely European permanent servants and officers, it became a Native community of provisioners, and permanent and seasonal workers.

At the time that York was evolving as a community of Native labourers and their families, the development of associated

---

15 The extent to which Native people engaged in activities outside the fur trade is a topic only recently addressed by fur-trade scholars. Complaints throughout the archival record by HBC officers that Indians were "lazy" or "improvident" in terms of trapping or voyaging to the post are being reinterpreted to demonstrate the Native people often followed different priorities that remained outside their participation in the trade. See Jennifer S.H. Brown, "The Blind Man and the Elephant: Fur Trade History Revisited," *Proceedings of the Fort Chipewyan and Fort Vermillion Bicentennial Conference*, ed. Patricia A. McCormack and R. Geoffrey Ironside (Edmonton: University of Alberta, Boreal Institute for Northern Studies 1990), 15–19.

institutions, such as the establishment of a Christian church and school, was taking place. Although a missionary had first visited York as early as 1820, the first permanent mission there was not established until the 1850s. A church and school served the local population until the post closed in 1957.

York Factory's decline after 1875 was to have severe and far-reaching effects upon the Cree people who lived at or near the post, or who had traditionally traded and taken debt there. As the company "restructured" its operations in the north, it reduced its demand for seasonal labour. This reduction coincided with a protracted decline in the population of fur-bearing animals in the Hayes-Nelson watershed after 1890, which resulted in much deprivation among the Native peoples of the area and the out-migration of many families to Split Lake, Churchill, and Norway House. Starvation became a reality for many of those who lived in the York district as HBC efforts to "rationalize" expenditures there – primarily by reducing Native debt – drove many to the bush and the vagaries of a land where game was increasingly scarce.[16]

By the turn of the century, however, competitive fur markets had re-emerged, largely because independent traders were now operating in the region. Better prices, coupled with the annuity payments guaranteed to the York Factory band under Treaty Five, helped to re-establish a more stable population of post servants and hunters and their families after 1910, although it was much reduced in numbers from the pre-1875 era. Fluctuating fur prices after 1920 affected the York Factory region, as did periodic supply shortages that reflected the seasonal cycle of local fur-bearing populations and the pressures on the carrying capacity of the district. The high prices for certain types of fur in the mid-1920s, in part caused by a shortage of supply and in part related to changing market demand and the influence of independent traders in the region, were soon followed by a steep plunge after

---

16 See Frank Tough, 'As Their Natural Resources Fail': Native Peoples and the Economic History of Northern Manitoba, 1870–1930 (Vancouver: UBC Press 1996), 63–74.

An aerial view of York Factory, 1925. (National Archives of Canada, Air Photo Library, F.A. 211.18).

1928. Values rebounded to some extent after 1935 and continued to rise until the early 1940s.[17]

The selection of York in 1911 as the company's headquarters for the Nelson River District helped to create an increased demand for Native labour at the post, although employment remained largely seasonal. Cree families continued their traditional seasonal movements based upon the subsistence cycle. For many, winters were spent at such small communities as Kaskatamagun, located east of York near the mouth of the Kaskattama River, while summers would find them at the post, trading, purchasing supplies, and providing part-time labour services. A much smaller population tended to stay at the post the year round and worked for the company there as full-time wage-earners. With the shifting of the Nelson River headquarters to Churchill in 1929, York Factory experienced a fairly rapid decline in both its economic profitability and its population. The company's decision to close the post in 1957 led to the relocation of the few remaining families to York Landing, Gillam, and other nearby communities. Many of these people sought work with the railway or with the mining and logging operations that had replaced the fur trade as the major resource-extraction industries in northern Manitoba. After almost three centuries, aboriginal–Euro-Canadian trade at the mouth of the Hayes River ended, and with it the long association of Cree peoples with York Factory.

If "official" written records provide one perspective on the lives of the York Factory Cree, the oral record allows for another, a direct voice that presents the social history of life experiences and everyday events. In presenting the recollections of ordinary people who were associated with York over the last four decades of its existence as a trading post – people whose lives are usually reduced to the almost statistical tabulation of historical and ethnographic surveys – we illustrate that historical reality is indeed multivocal. As a component of social history, oral traditions can reveal how people comprehend and attempt to make sense of the

---

17 See Frank Tough, "*Native People and the Regional Economy of Northern Manitoba, 1870–1930s*" (PHD dissertation, York University 1987), 322–408.

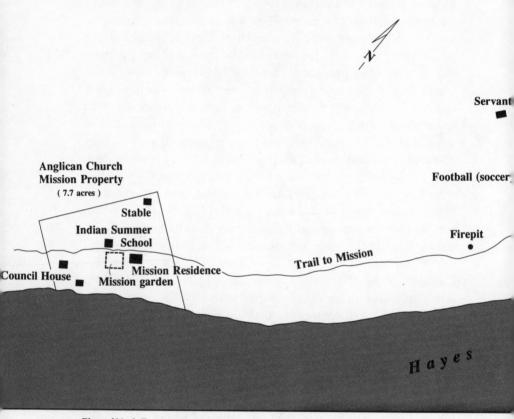

Plan of York Factory, *c.* 1930.

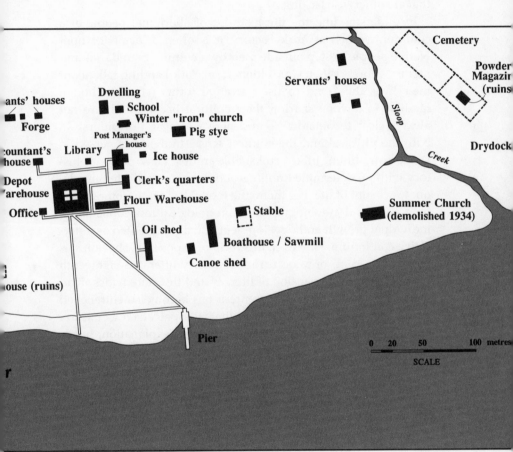

ants' houses

Forge

Dwelling

School

Winter "iron" church

Servants' houses

Cemetery

Powder
Magazin
(ruins

Sloop

Post Manager's
house

Pig stye

ountant's
house

Library

Ice house

Clerk's quarters

Creek

Drydock

Depot
arehouse

Flour Warehouse

Office

Stable

Summer Church
(demolished 1934)

Oil shed

Boathouse / Sawmill

ouse (ruins)

Canoe shed

Pier

r

0   20   50   100 metres

SCALE

upheavals they have experienced, such as new religious beliefs, technological changes, personal tragedy, and alterations to age-old patterns of subsistence and migration. Their stories substantially alter the focus of historical inquiries, opening perspectives that are otherwise lacking.

In understanding the life histories of aboriginal people at a community such as York Factory, it is often difficult for non-Native people to step outside their own cultural boundaries and literary genres. When Cree elders from York Landing talk about their lives they tend to use narrative forms which, although familiar to anyone sharing their cultural background, are not always clear to outsiders – and here we mean "outsiders" in both the physical and the cultural sense. Individuals versed in Western tradition, Julie Cruikshank argues, view personal history with predetermined notions about what constitutes an adequate account of life. For them, the model has come from written biography and autobiography – chronological reflections about individual growth and development usually presented as a narrative continuum. However, this form of exposition, she notes, is relatively recent, only occurring regularly after the eighteenth century with the expansion of literacy and the more widespread use of the written text. As a genre it has become so entrenched and so structured by convention that it is perceived as natural and an approach that not only requires no explanation, but is considered the sole acceptable way of writing personal history.[18]

For Cree elders from York Factory, descriptions of past events and experiences rely upon an oral tradition that is deeply rooted in local idiom and vernacular speech. Traditional tales, mythology, references to places of importance not found on any map, second-hand apocryphal accounts, funny stories, and commonplace events often take on a greater significance in the oral accounts of the Cree than they do in Western forms of autobiography and are often the shared aspects of life that provide continuity between generations.

Although oral history can furnish new perspectives and new sources of information, it has often been criticized for being

---

18 Cruikshank, *Life Lived like a Story*, ix.

overly subjective and biased. Sceptics argue that memory is selective and often not reliable; that the interview situation may dis-
tort recollections; or that individual interviews are often not
representative. Oral history, however, is not a separate branch of
history, but is a method to be used together with other sources.
Photographs, written records, and data about material culture
provide a more complete picture when they are combined with
the oral record. And while oral history has its biases, so do all
other forms of historical documentation, including the government report, the fur-trade journal, the photograph, the archaeological find, and even the census book.

The construction of a particular version of history requires
more than simply understanding how and why certain types
of historical documents were generated. The integrity of the
research process itself is central to an honest and adequate por-
trayal of the past. This issue is particularly acute in the gathering
of oral testimonies, where the sorts of questions asked and the
selection of material for publication can easily skew the recollections of the individual who speaks into the microphone. At the
commencement of the York Factory Oral History Project we for-
mulated a number of general questions that touched on a wide
range of topics relating to life in the region. These questions were
largely designed to serve as guidelines to facilitate conversation
and provide a broad structure for the interviews. Recognizing
our own biases and limitations, we attempted to keep the interviews as open as possible so that respondents had free rein to
discuss the topics of greatest interest to them. The results were
illuminating, for the elders provided recollections that were
thoughtful, candid, and sometimes surprising. The subjects covered at times followed the direction of the questions; at other
times they led into new and revealing areas about work and daily
life, recreation, survival, and traditional knowledge.

The interviewer was Flora Beardy, a Cree speaker born at Kaskatamagun and raised at York Factory. Either related or known
to many of the elders who spoke with her, Flora was able to es-
tablish a bond of trust with each individual which resulted in
conversations that were for the most part relaxed and open.
Often people were as eager to share their stories with Flora as
they were to see these reminiscences made available to others.

The trust between Flora and the elders was central to the success of the endeavour. Her own deep personal commitment to the project honoured and respected this trust and went a long way in helping to create a collection of unique personal documents about the lives of the Cree people of York Factory.

Some comments about translation are necessary. All of the interviews were conducted in the Cree language and were later translated and transcribed into English by Flora Beardy. As much as possible the English text is a literal translation of the spoken Cree, although at times the phrasing was slightly altered in an attempt to make the English more comprehensible to readers. A translation of the English into Cree syllabics is planned so that those elders from York Factory who read neither English nor roman-orthography Cree will be able to read their own stories in their traditional written language.

Beyond the challenges of language and translation, another issue arises when converting an oral tradition to a written text: the problem of the perceived authority of the written word over the spoken. Writing down the oral accounts of the York Factory elders as we have done in this book is not intended to supplant storytelling as an oral tradition, nor does it privilege these accounts over others. Rather, it is a way of sharing them with a wider audience in a format that is easily understood by people familiar with the written tradition. By depositing the original tapes with the Provincial Archives of Manitoba and making copies available to the elders and their families as well as to the governments of the various First Nations, we hope to keep these oral traditions in their spoken form alive and accessible.

Many hours of recordings were made throughout the course of the project and each interview was translated and transcribed in its entirety. Faced with the restrictions on length imposed by the realities of publishing, we were forced to select portions for use in the book. In doing so we adhered to no hard and fast criteria, instead trying as best we could to choose material that we felt was representative of the interview as a whole. This process was by nature a subjective one – certain accounts were chosen over others for their representativeness, their clarity, and their illustrative value – but it was guided by the principle of integrity and a desire to preserve the confidence of each interviewee.

What is lost in writing down and selecting oral testimonies for publication, however, is the tonal quality of the interview itself; the character and pitch of the voice, the richness of oral and vernacular expression, or simply the nature of conversation where pauses, gestures, and facial expressions convey meaning that is beyond the communicative powers of the written word. We endeavoured to maintain the conversational tone and style by minimizing the number of changes to the transcript. Grammatical errors in the translation reflect the colloquial quality of the original spoken Cree. Square-bracketed insertions, which provide the names of people mentioned in the text as simply "he" or "she," or which are used to make short explanatory notations, were added sparingly. Punctuation was also employed to improve the flow of the text and ellipsis points were occasionally inserted to indicate where sentences or parts of sentences were omitted. Except in a handful of instances where their inclusion was essential to understanding the nature and context of the response, the interview questions were left out of the edited transcripts. This choice was made partly to sustain the readability of the narrative and partly because the selected material did not always come out of a direct enquiry by the interviewer. As well, many of the questions asked by Flora – "Can you tell me about your childhood?" or "What kind of work did you do for the Hudson's Bay Company?" – were of a general nature and the substance of the answers tended to make the actual question if not redundant, then at least self-evident. Rather than reproduce the questions, we chose to organize the responses under eighteen subheadings. In the written transcripts certain themes emerged that were common to many of the interviews, although individual recollections often provided different perspectives. Attitudes toward the HBC at York Factory, or the fairness of the company's fur prices, for example, varied among the elders. In the end we felt that the grouping of responses under these subheadings managed to capture the essence of each interview while maintaining the narrative quality of the text.

The texts are supplemented by occasional endnotes to provide the reader with information on specific points such as the location of certain geographical features or the background of historical personalities. The notes also offer context for topics raised in the narratives, often giving comparative examples or tracing historical phenomena to an earlier period at York Factory. They rely heavily upon documentary and published sources and are intended only to complement the oral narratives, not as correctives to the recollections of the elders. Both forms of documentation, the oral and the written, speak for themselves.

A number of photographs were lent to us by the elders and others for reproduction in the book. They illustrate aspects of daily life at York Factory in the twentieth century and are published here for the first time. Additional photographs from archival repositories are also included.

Through these oral accounts and autobiographical stories, the York Factory elders have provided insights into a way of life that has largely disappeared in northern Manitoba. The era that they describe and were part of, namely the years between 1920 and the closing of the post in 1957, saw dramatic transformations in aboriginal life in the north. The extension of Treaty Five in 1910 to include members of the York Factory band, the arrival of police and government agents, and the changing economy of the fur trade all had their impacts, both good and bad, on the lives of the Cree people who resided along the western shore of Hudson Bay. But these accounts also depict the continuity of northern life in the twentieth century, from the persistence of traditional ways to the ongoing role of community and kinship ties. The stories are more than recollections of a distant past. They are a legacy to a younger generation of aboriginal people whose present reality is both forward-looking and informed by the past. In this sense the York Factory elders who speak in this book are teachers in the truest meaning of the word.

Robert Coutts
Winnipeg, Manitoba

Voices from Hudson Bay

Alex Spence after a goose hunt at York Factory, *c.* 1930s. (Courtesy of Flora Beardy).

Voices from Hudson Bay

TRADERS, TRIPPERS, AND TRAPPERS

John Neepin. In the summer, all summer, they [my family] would set nets for fish. They'd check the nets when the tide goes out. They would put up some poles, in a row, and attach the net to them. Then after the tide goes out they'd go and remove the fish from the nets. Later on, as I got older, I was able to help them. I would go and set nets. When we were old enough to travel with our father we would go and stay northward of Port Nelson. This place is called *Asiniy Sîpiy* [Stony River]. This is where we always went. This is where I grew up and became a man. That's where we fished and trapped. We were there for the winters. Then I left there. I left there in 1941. I've been on the railroad since. Seventy-six ... yes, 1976 was when I stopped working for Canadian National Railways.

This is one thing that I remember, that I find strange. I often think of this. Why the people aren't allowed to hunt any time. We are allowed to hunt only at certain times. This doesn't make things any better for the wildlife. That's just like having a garden and not tending to it. If this garden is not looked after properly all that would grow in it would be weeds. God put all these animals on earth for the people to use. And today they stop people from hunting.[1] I hear a lot of people say that the geese don't taste as good as they used to.

We were taught certain ways of hunting. People weren't allowed to build a fire at night. We weren't allowed to hunt after dark or when it was calm. A person wasn't allowed to do this.[2]

I was taught very well by the old man [*kisê-ininiw*] that taught me. He taught me everything about hunting. We were taught to never wear anything red. Especially when we were hunting geese. The geese are afraid of the colour red. And today I believe that. That last time I was hunting at York Factory, I had to come around the point. Anyway, there were all these geese flying in all directions! It was calm that day. It looked like they were afraid of something. An Indian can tell when the geese are afraid. They act differently when they are not afraid. They take their time flying. That's how you can tell. But these ones were all excited. [The hunters] were dressed in red clothing! That's what the geese do when they see the colour red.

At Kaskatamagun there was a big group of people living there. People survived by trapping. Sometimes they would come to York Factory during the winter if they ran short of supplies. They would bring their fur to sell. Then the same person would arrive again at Easter with more fur to sell. I don't think the Hudson's Bay Company paid a fair price. But then, in turn, things weren't very expensive at that time. For instance, when I first took a fox pelt to sell I received ten dollars for it. That was the highest price paid and the same with mink. It was worth ten dollars. But later on the fur prices went higher. They paid more for fur but then the prices for food items also went up. There was no difference.

The Hudson's Bay Company encouraged people to take cash on credit. If the people didn't have money they were able to get it from the Hudson's Bay Company, on credit.

I never trapped beaver. When I started trapping nobody was allowed to trap beaver. Beaver was closed all the time I trapped! The odd time I would trap one. Secretly. For food.

The geese were hunted every spring. The powder was kept in barrels. There would be a person in charge of this gunpowder. They would have a barrel and a little dipper/cup. It was called a one one-hundreth scoop ... If you got one scoop that was enough for ten geese! So if you got ten scoops that was enough for a person to get a hundred geese! Yes! Some did get a hundred but some only got fifty. And again some only got twenty-five! There were also some who did not kill any geese at all! That's what I used to hear. The ones that were good hunters usually had some gunpowder left. Some of the ten scoops that they received. One of

Goose hunters at York Factory, *c*. 1940. *Left to right:* Johnny Gibeault, Alex Spence, Charlie Bland, Hector Spence, and Isiah Saunders. (Courtesy of Flora Beardy).

Jake Spence, Hector Spence, and Alex Spence, 1946. (Provincial Archives of Manitoba, Malaher Collection, 41).

our grandfathers use to tell us that he used all of his in one day of hunting! He had received ten scoops of gunpowder. He said that towards the evening, he thought he was hallucinating/dreaming because of all the geese he got. He got a hundred geese! Yes. He was proud when he brought in all his geese.

The number taken [of geese] was usually to feed the people over a period of time. This is what we did also at Port Nelson. We hunted enough to last the summer. We didn't go and hunt all the time. When we needed more food then we'd go hunt. Sometimes we were able to keep the geese in barrels over the summer. It didn't take long to fill the barrels. They weren't very big. Yes, sometimes this was done but the geese didn't taste very good this way because they were packed in salt.

When a person talks about the great number of polar bears there are today he would say, "That's what my father probably thought when he talked about the polar bears being numerous." My father used to talk about this, and this is what he said. I guess there were lots of polar bears during the time his grandfather was a young man! So it's probably the same thing today. This is what my father used to tell me. He said the bears never used to bother anyone. Even though there were bears around we never heard of one killing a human. To kill a person, we never heard of this happening. There was another old man that used to tell us that he, too, never heard of a bear killing a person. Today, I hear of this happening. It's probably because they [scientists, researchers, and conservation officers] bother the bears so much. The drug that these animals receive is probably what's causing their strange behaviour. And also the collars they put on them. This must cause them some distress. They are not used to this. They are distressed from these drugs and collars. A lot of these animals must get sick and irritated.

Well that's what this polar bear did at Mile 412 [on the railway line]. No one saw this bear because it came during the night. It was David Massan who saw the tracks the next morning. So he followed the tracks. He said he didn't have to go too far. He knew he was close when he heard sounds coming from the bear. They were distress/hurting sounds. He went a bit closer and saw this bear rolling around, and the bear had its head in its paws. It was holding its head and rolling around. The bear was acting crazy, not normal. This bear was obviously suffering and acting very strange. We all know that it is wrong to make animals suffer. There are some people who come and ask me about the animals. Some don't realize how important these animals were to us and to our forefathers. They have to be respected. I really wish that they would understand this. One white man asked me what good the animals were to the Indians! I told him that we use the animals the way a white man uses his gardens. For food. And for clothing! The white man cares for his garden to feed his family and the Indian cares for the animals for the same reasons.

That's the one thing I'm not happy about and I feel like this because I know this person couldn't seem to understand how important these animals were and still are, to us. Our grandfathers never abused the use of these animals and they didn't check on other people. If food was needed they would go and hunt for it. People ate what they liked to eat. The Indians took and used what they needed. Nobody told them they couldn't. That is the way it was with the Indians, a long time ago, when it came to hunting. They didn't kill for the fun of it and they didn't take more than they needed. They didn't overkill. They took enough to last for awhile and then hunted again when more was needed. These traditions were taught and passed on from generation to generation. Strangers were also told this. Not to overkill. I was taught this. That's why we have all these animals and birds. I often think about these creatures. Today we are only allowed to hunt them at certain times and in limited amounts. It can't be too good for them if there are too many. The garden is worked on and looked after all the time. That's how it produces food. When this food is removed, it is replanted again so it will produce more food. Now our animals that we are not allowed to hunt will be overpopulated. We don't really know if that is good for their well-being.[3] These creatures were put on this earth to be used by the people.

It's not too long ago that the geese have started arriving early. Soon as it warms up they start arriving. That's just recently this is happening. It wasn't like that a long time ago. Never. I come from that area [York Factory and Port Nelson] so I know. I grew up there. I was brought up on geese. They never arrived early. We always waited for them and they would not come until May. The word that we use for the geese in the spring, *mâtâw-ispanihowak*, means "flying through in great flocks." They are coming from the south. These geese fly along the coast. But there are geese that will stay in the area and nest. There is another word for the ones that stay for a short while and then leave for the north: *sipwêwi-sakamipaniwak* means "flying over the coastline." And then, again, in the fall when they arrive the word is *akwânâwak* which means "driven by the wind." They are flying with the wind and driven to shore.[4]

Mary Redhead. He [Mary's father, David Neepin] would trap in the winter. That's how he made his money. That's what he did. There were no jobs then. Everyone lived off the land. They would trap and sell the pelts. Maybe they saved some money for emergencies, like if they ran short of food. They probably had their money in the store, ready for them to use when they needed it.

Alex Ouscan [David Neepin's partner] would be the first one to return with a full bag of geese. My father sent him ahead so Elizabeth [Alex's mother, Elizabeth Ouscan] can prepare some. Then cook some and feed the children.

We used to do some trapping too. My older sister Jessie and I. We would trap snowy owls with traps! We would go to a clearing. I was just learning. Jessie was good at this. I was just learning from her! She set two traps and told me that the closest one was mine. She caught one first in her trap. I started running towards the owl. I was going to pet it! She yelled at me to stop. She said: "Watch out! The owl will scratch you!" That's how stupid I was! I was going to grab the owl and pet it. She would drive a stick into the ground to secure the trap, then cover the trap with grass. When the owl lands on the grass it gets caught in the trap. Oh yes! People ate them. They ate the owls! They're good eating. I remember when people use to eat seagulls too. But they don't eat them today.

[Today] they don't want anyone to set nets [in the Bird and Gillam areas]. They don't want anyone to fish because you can't eat it. The fish have something in them that can make a person ill.[5] Take the beaver. Before, the beaver was very good. It used to taste real good. Now today, I don't know what it tastes like. It tastes awful! It sure doesn't taste like it did in the past. I hear lots of people say this. They say the beaver tastes awful!

Richard Beardy. At one time [silver fox] pelts were worth $700 for one! Then it came down to $500. Then the Hudson's Bay Company started raising these foxes. Sometimes when a person asked for a live fox they were given one! But later on the prices came down because there were just too many of these foxes. The Hudson's Bay Company couldn't keep up with the high prices so they lowered it. That's what happened with this fox.[6]

From what I remember there used to be lots of caribou towards this way. Where the Hayes and Nelson Rivers are, there used to be a place called *Tastawic* [Halfway Place] and not far from there was a lake. There used to be caribou there. Also on this other side, east of here, along the coast.[7] For geese we didn't have to go far to get them. They were always around here.

If they [hunters] were going to go their own way then they would go alone but most of the time it was in groups. Take for instance Kaskatamagun. This was a good place. It provided lots of wild game, birds, which meant food for the people, and food meant survival! It was a life-giving place.

David Massan. [To make a wooden trap] you get some sticks and stand them on each side but you have to know the width of the animal that you're going to trap. You use that for measurement. That's where you stand the sticks up. The other sticks are set in a way to support the weight of another big stump. When the animal moved the main support stick, then the rest of the stump would fall on it, trapping or holding it down. A string is also used. It is tied among the logs, then set inside the wooden trap. When the animal pulls the bait on the string, this pulls the support stick/beam, causing the rest of the logs to fall on the animal.

If it's a big animal that you're trapping, your log on the top will be a lot heavier and larger. You have to build it strong, so it doesn't break, especially where the bait is set. It should be strong and sturdy. The old people, whenever they set rabbit snares, would take some of the rabbit droppings, and rub it all over the string to be used for a snare. Then they would say as they are rubbing the string: "Don't chew on the snare string. You'll die if you eat your own droppings! So don't chew on the string!" Yes, this is what they used to do. Also I don't remember seeing too many people with fishing nets. Maybe just a few. People depended on weirs for their fish. They would build weirs and trap the fish.

That's what they survived on. Oh, there used to be lots of fish caught in these weirs.[8] People would just throw the fish out onto the riverbank! They used the weirs until the river started freezing. That's when they had to be on guard, at this time of year. When the boxes filled up they would freeze together if no one was there to take them out. These boxes used to fill up so fast – that's how much fish there was. Some fish were kept in the water and a net was used to pull them ashore. They were usually stored for the winter so the people wouldn't go hungry.

Fred Beardy. Yes, we didn't waste anything. One stage of cleaning the moose hide is using the brain. You take the brain out and rub it on the hide to soften it. You do the same thing to caribou skins. The skins were used for a lot of things and were not wasted. Even today we still use them. Sometimes we'll bring back whole hides and people here will take them and prepare them. The moose hide is tough and durable. From the hides we cut out strips to make our snowshoe webbing.

Alex Ouscan. At that same time [early 1920s] there were lots of white foxes.[9] Lots of them! They were all over the place. They all came from the north. Lots of them. They came during the night. At that time, people didn't know to set snares for them. Their tracks were all along the shore, close to the waterline. All around there! And nobody knew to set snares. They would have caught lots. When one fox got caught in the trap the other foxes would kill it! The next morning, when the trap was checked, there would be nothing but fur left! The other foxes would eat the trapped one.

Joseph Saunders. In the fall, when the trappers set out, they would charge up what they need. I also saw them get a canoe and charge that. I also saw some purchase guns, sometimes two guns, and put it on credit.[10]

It was my father that told me how much they got for fur pelts a long time ago. The one they call a marten – well, at that time, money value was measured in pelts, such as one full pelt or one half pelt. The marten was worth one half beaver pelt and in today's money value, about 25 cents [dollars?]. This was the marten's value. The white fox also had the same value: one half beaver.[11]

Amy Hill. I myself used to snare rabbits. My young child would be in the cradle and I'd carry the cradle on my back. This way I'd have the baby with me while I set rabbit snares. Early the next morning I'd go check the snares. Then I'd have to carry the rabbits back along with the baby. I'd put the rabbits on my back and then put the cradle on top! This is what I did in order to survive, to have food for the children. This was when he [Amy's husband, Albert] was away checking his traps and setting other ones. He'd usually go further up-river from the main camp. Yes, lots of times this is what I did. I also had to get my own wood.

The rabbit skin was prepared and then used for clothing. It was used for blankets too. I made a blanket from rabbit skins. You need lots to make a big blanket! You sew them together. First you take the rabbit skin and flesh it properly. Then it's washed and dried. You cut it into strips and braid the strips and then these are sewn together to make the blanket. You have to braid the strips because the rabbit skin tears easily.

Richard Beardy. To make a living the people would do all sorts of things, sometimes even work for the Hudson's Bay Company. Fishing was the most important source of survival during the summer. They would put the net out in the river with people at each end and slowly drag it to shore, catching the fish as they dragged the net.[12] At that time we had nice, strong dogs and we took good care of them. Fish was their main source of food. Dogs were very important then.

David Massan. The whales were also used for dog food. That's what we used when I was at Port Nelson. They used to catch them. Sometimes we would get three in one net. Then we'd drag them to shore. We rendered the oil from them. They have thick skins, maybe the thickness of my wrist. Sometimes we'd get a twenty-gallon drum full of oil. This would last all winter.[13] The meat is put into a barrel and buried in the ground. This was for the dogs. You would just take some as you need it. Same with the seals. We do the same thing. We cut it up, hide and all.

We used to travel to and trap in different areas along the coast. Come up the coast towards the Owl River area. I used to go with Moses Neepin. His trapline was between Port Nelson and Owl River. When we travelled the women would walk along the shore

York Factory Cree workers and hunters with beluga whale carcass, *c.* 1890.
(National Archives of Canada, Geological Survey of Canada Collection, NA 39935).

and we would be in the boat. They worked hard. The women would walk and also pack loads on their back. When the tide was in we'd pull to shore and make camp. Robert and his family too. Robert Miles. That's who I travelled with, most of the time. At first I travelled with Moses Neepin, then Robert. We went all the way to Owl River. They used to use whaling boats to travel in. These were big boats. Coast boats.[14] They were hard to handle if it was windy. If they weren't properly anchored, the wind and tide could easily carry them out. One time a big wind came up. We were on shore and Robert stayed in the boat out in the bay. Sometimes we couldn't see him because of the waves. With these boats, if too much water got into them they'd sink! He didn't want to lose his boat so he stayed out there and looked after it.

Albert Hill. The other thing used for dog food was the white whales. They also made whale oil. You know those barrels, the forty-five-gallon drums? These are the ones he would fill with whale oil. These barrels were called whale pots.

Wherever a family made camp, a net would be set to catch fish. Snares were set for rabbits. This would be done after camp was made and the tent was all set up. Setting snares, the different ways of obtaining food, was how a person survived. These were the most two important food sources for the families: fish and rabbits.

Amy Hill. The bears make dens north of the York Factory area. On this side [pointing] and again north of the Kaskatamagun area. They'll go where there's trees and lots of snow and they'll have their cubs there. She'll stay in that area. She won't bring her cubs to the ice until they get a little bigger. She's to be feared at this time because of the cubs. They're smart!

The Indians used to kill the seals and use the meat for good food. They would take the sealskin. This skin would be softened and then they made harnesses for the dogs. I used to see my late father do this.

Archelaus Beardy. In the fall we would catch a lot of ciscoes.[15] Well, at this time of the year [prior to freeze-up] the fish don't go to the bottom of the river. They hang around the grass, close to

Buying furs at York Factory, 1923. (Hudson's Bay Company Archives, Provincial
Archives of Manitoba).

the top and also close to shore. By this time it's getting cold. Towards fall and this is when we would fish. We would have this long net with floats on one side and weights on the other. A couple of guys would stay on shore with one end and a couple would go out on the water, by canoe, with the other end. Then we would drag the net back to shore, catching the fish as we went along.

My father took fifty skins to the Hudson's Bay Company. All prime pelts. He got twenty-five dollars for one. For the dark foxes they paid thirty-five dollars for one. This is where all the fur was taken, to the Hudson's Bay Company store.[16] Here they were pressed and packed into bales and then they were put on the ship. The furs were kept in storage until they were put on the ship. These bales were loaded on the ship. The fur came from Shamattawa (there was a Hudson's Bay Company store there) and also came from Kaskatamagun. These pelts were brought to York Factory. It was at York Factory that they made the bales. These were heavy bales.

Amy Hill. When we lived at York Factory, there was already some sort of mosquito repellent to protect ourselves. As for my mother and father, during the summer whenever they checked their snares, they would carry a pail with them. Inside the pail is earth and when this is lit it produces smoke! That's how they protected themselves. The smoke kept the mosquitoes away. In the wigwam they would put earth into the fire to make smoke. This certain kind of earth didn't burn; it just made smoke. This was usually placed in the doorway also to keep out the mosquitoes.[17]

Abel Chapman. He [Abel's grandfather, Chief Abraham Beardy] looked after me, most of my childhood. My father didn't take me until I was sixteen. At times there was just my grandmother [Sally Beardy] and I at home. All the rest of the family left for winter trapping [including] Archelaus and Richard.[18] Lots of times I set out with my grandmother. She would go set some traps. I was young but I was able to walk on snowshoes. My grandmother used to carry a rabbit skin. Do you know what I mean? In this skin she would wrap some meat, already cooked, and some bannock. The lunch would never freeze. No, it wouldn't freeze.

Sometimes she would kill two minks, but she would get lots of weasels.

There's one animal the people didn't like and it was the bravest of all the animals. This animal would go into the camps and steal food. It's the wolverine, or the thief! He was a terrible animal. The Indians lost a lot to this animal. He even would steal from the traps! Steal the bait and also tear the animals that are caught in the trap. Anything that was caught in the traps. He'd eat the animals. Foxes, minks. I think the only animal it couldn't get was the otter [because] the traps were set in the water. He was the animal despised by all the Indians. A person cannot eat whatever the wolverine leaves behind. It will piss all over the carcass so nobody else can eat it! That's what they say about this animal. That's how evil the wolverine is. It is not a well-liked animal.[19]

When I was first trapping, the nicest mink you can get, the largest size, was worth five dollars. This is how much it was worth. This was when I first started. I must have been sixteen years old then. I was able then to go by myself. I never went with anybody else. I walked all over by myself. And for an otter, I received fifteen dollars. That's all I got. For a beaver skin, it was the same. Yes, for an extra-large beaver pelt, I think they paid twenty dollars. That's what I got. The price of the [arctic] white fox never changed. The price stayed the same. Each pelt was worth twenty-five dollars. Even if the pelt was smaller than normal, it was still worth the same. This is what my father used to tell me also. One season he trapped a hundred white foxes during one winter, and also my wife's mother, she too trapped a hundred foxes and also Sammy, Sammy Saunders was his name.

I used to hear people say that the "money fox" or "silver fox" was worth a lot of money. Some quoted the price as five hundred dollars for one pelt.

We had spent the winter at Port Nelson. Then we left there, my family. We moved to this place called *Nootawan Sîpiy*, north of Port Nelson. We left Port Nelson in September and I didn't see any other Indians until Christmas! I was all alone, trapping. My father-in-law [Moses Neepin] was trapping alone also around the same area but we didn't see each other. We didn't go back until Christmas. At that time I never thought of being lonely. There wasn't anybody else around. The only companions I had were the dogs. At this time there were lots of caribou. Oh my! Lots of them! We travelled towards Owl River,[20] to this little river and from there we turned around and came back. We stayed there for three days, trapping. *Asikoopetitawapoi* is what this place is called. I don't know. *Asikoopetitawapoi* is what it was called [when] my father-in-law used to live and trap there. There's the Owl River and Port Nelson. This place is about half way [between the two]. So on our way back we camped at this place called *Wapinayo Sîpiy.*[21] This was on our way back to *Nootawan Sîpiy.* That's the name of this place. We arrived there, made camp, and when I was sleeping I had a dream. I dreamt we were going to this place of many white men, so many that you couldn't pass through them. So after I woke up I said to my later father-in-law: "I wonder what this dream means? I dreamt that where we're going to, there were lots of white men – so many that you can't pass through them. I wonder what this means?" He didn't answer me. So the next day at sunrise we left for Port Nelson. We reached this place where there's a big clearing and oh, you should have seen the sight that greeted us! Caribou. Lots of them! So many that you couldn't see through them! Close to us! Some would run off to the side for a short distance and stop. They would be short of breath. Later they didn't bother running away but at first they were afraid. As we moved along they would just move apart and make room for us.

WORK AND WAGES

David Massan. I used to work. I would load and unload supplies. We would work when the ships came in, unloading.[22] That was hard work and the pay wasn't very much. We would work all day. Some of the supplies were really heavy to lift. The company would also feed us while we worked. Canned food, biscuits, and tea. When we loaded supplies for the [York] boat going to Shamattawa, that's when we worked hard. We would go along with the boat to Shamattawa. We would have to drag the boat along the shore. One boat carried 800 pounds. The other boat was larger and older and it carried 1,000 pounds. We would drag the boat. This was in the summer, and it was real hot and there were

lots of mosquitoes! And we would have to paddle the boat there
and back. The oars we used were big ones. We would have to
stand up to use them.[23]

Archelaus Beardy. It was usually just us that worked here [in the
depot building]. William Beardy, Elijah Beardy, George Spence,
Simeon Spence, Stephen Beardy, and myself. Our job was to clean
around and under the depot building. The mud collected so
much under the floorboards that at times it came through the
floor even though the building was sitting on big, wooden logs.[24]
That's how much mud there was under the building. We cleaned
everything up. Mud and all. We would carry it out in a wooden
box and dump it at the riverbank. It would take two of us to carry
the crateful of mud and the riverbank was quite a distance away.
We would start work at 6:00 A.M. and finish at 6:00 P.M. and our
pay was $3.50 per day.

John Neepin. This one elder was talking to us and, at that time, we
were getting paid with money. We were collecting our pay and
we each received a lot of money. Anyway, he went on to say:
"You're all happy right now, receiving these large amounts of
money. Not long from now we'll all be facing new hardships. The
prices of everything will rise and as this happens, it will be hard
for everyone. For all of you." This I always remember him saying
and now I believe it! It has come true. Take this cigarette package,
for instance. It used to cost 25 cents. Now, today, if you pay six
dollars for a package you get two cents back. That's all. Now I
know what he was talking about. He was right!

Catherine Anderson. At an early age I learned how to sew and do
beadwork. This was also how I earned money. From sewing. My
stepmother didn't sew very much. She did some but not very
much. I did most of it. We didn't do any sewing while we were
away. When we got back from the trapline, then I would do all
the sewing.

Albert Hill. The women used to sew. They sewed all the time. Remember they used to have a group of women who did sewing.
There would be one woman in charge of this group. One woman

Sawing lumber at York Factory, 1930s. (Courtesy of John Ingram).

was the boss. Just like yourself [Flora Beardy]. You're in charge of what you are doing today. Collecting our stories. That's how it was with this group. One woman was in charge. They were known as the group of women who sewed. They would do bead-work.

Amy Hill. Make moccasins.

Albert Hill. Dresses made of caribou hide.

Amy Hill. Vests.

Albert Hill. They'd put beads on them. Then after these items were completed then they sell them. All the items that were sewn were sold. They made money. They also had one person who looked after the money that was received from selling these hand-icrafts. The money would be used for different purposes. If a family was short of food some of the money would be used to buy food, or if there was a death in one's family and they needed some financial assistance then some money would be available for this.

Fred Beardy. We built this goose camp, in the York Factory area, in 1970. This is the one at Ten Shilling [Creek] and I started working there in 1972. I worked with John Hatley[25] then and I think that's fifteen summers I worked there. If all goes well I'll go again this year [1989]. He's already written to me asking me to come and work again. It's not hard work, just when you kill a moose. We start off guiding fishermen, then we go into the goose-hunting season, and when that's over we're into moose-hunting season. We go up the river about eighty miles. This is the Hayes River. We go about eighty or eighty-five miles. This is where the moose camp is.

Abel Chapman. My late father worked [for the HBC]. They would leave after the rivers opened. He usually travelled with late William Gray and George Spence. They would be gone for one month. Sometimes there were three of them. They carried straight mail, no other supplies. That's where they went to pick up mail [at Norway House]. This was done in winter also. He was the man who had this job, to go and get mail at Norway House. Soon as travelling was good, then he'd leave, pulling his sled. He would leave in November, around the fifteenth. Then he'd be back at Christmas.

Oh, it was a busy time [when the ship arrived at York Factory]! They'd have a dance. That's the truth! They would have a dance right away. Yes, they unloaded the boat, and then towards evening is when the dance started.[26] My father used to tell us a story of a bad HBC boss at York Factory. He said he was called *Kihci-pôcôw*. That's what they called him! He said he wasn't a very good boss. I guess at this time my grandfather was already a chief, Abraham [Beardy]. Anyway during the unloading of the supplies even the children helped. They helped as much as they could. They'd unload what they were able to carry. I guess my grandfather went to this boss, Mr *Pôcôw*. That's what they called him! I guess he asked him if he had already paid the children. So he said "Yes, I gave them one biscuit each." That's all he gave the children for the work they did! He said "Yes! I gave them one biscuit." My father went on to say that this fellow went to Fort Severn. He was the same over there and that's when they let him go. He [his father] said that he went to Fort Severn, at that time. He was on the same boat, coming back to York Factory. This one day it was time for all the men to eat. I guess this fellow also came forward to eat but he was told that he couldn't eat there! That he no longer had a job with the company. They found out what he was doing. The company let him go. Anyway, I guess he just sat there with his head down. I guess the minister, Mr Faries was also travelling with them. I guess Mr Faries said nobody wanted to feed him. No one wanted to help him. I guess he was looking at him sitting there and said to him: "See what has happened to you. This is because you don't care for anyone but yourself." I guess this is what he told this fellow. This man didn't move. He just sat there with his head down. They sent him away. They didn't want to feed him. He took advantage of the Indians. Lots of people left from the York Factory area because he wouldn't give them enough food, this Mr *Pôcôw*. They often went hungry because they didn't have enough food.

YORK BOATS, COAST BOATS, AND STEAMERS

Archelaus Beardy. The goods would come in [to York Factory] by boat and the boat that brought in the goods had sails on it. It was

Josiah Beardy (standing) manœuvring a York boat, n.d. (Courtesy of John Ingram).

Loading the schooner at York Factory, 1930s. (Courtesy of John Ingram).

a big boat and it came from far away.[27] It would anchor out in the bay, quite a ways from York Factory. That's where all the goods were unloaded from. They used wooden boats [to unload], the same wooden boats my father built, York boats. They also used smaller, light canoes. We used to get candies, but I never see those kind of candies today. They were a good size and they tasted real good!

Joseph Saunders. Oh yes, at first Mr Ray would bring his wares from this way [referring to the railway]. They probably came in on the train [to Gillam]. Then they used horses to take the goods to the last set of rapids that are called *Opâciwan* rapids. This is where he would haul them from here, in the summer, by canoe. His business was starting to do really good. A schooner would come into Wanatawahak/Crooked Bank from Moosonee, loaded with goods for Mr Ray's store. Then, not long after, the Hudson's Bay Company bought his store.[28]

Before the schooner, a sailboat was the boat that was used. It brought cargo to Kaskatamagun and it made two trips. This was in the fall of 1923. It was from here on that there was always supplies and a manager in the store. Before this some supplies were brought in during the summer. Not very much was brought in because there was no manager. The people would just help themselves to what they needed, when they needed them. In the winter, a manager would come in by dog team from York Factory. Dogs were also used to carry cargo in the winter. This is what they used to do at that time.

It was in the late fall when this boat came in. That's why it ran aground. It was snowing quite a bit. This boat use to anchor quite a ways out past Kaskatamagun. Sometimes closer to Mistikokan River, which is about twenty-five miles away.[29] We had to use York boats unloading it. First there were schooners, and then the coal boat *Mooswa*. My late father[30] used to work on this boat. There was one white man, who drove the boat, and one Indian. Old Rabiscah was the guy's name who used to keep the fire going on the boat.[31] Actually they were finished loading. All the boat had to do was leave. At that time, there was another boat there all set to sail. Well, this was when a big wind came up from the north. A strong wind! The guys on the schooner managed to get off but

not the ones on the *Mooswa*. The wind was so strong that it broke
the mooring lines on the *Mooswa*. The captain on the schooner,
not the head captain; they used to have two on the schooner, one
to drive the boat plus the head captain. Anyway, this captain
tried to reach the *Mooswa* but couldn't and the *Mooswa* couldn't
reach the schooner because the wind was too strong. They just
kept going and the waves were pretty high. A lot of water was
getting into the boat which finally put the fire [in the boilers] out
and the *Mooswa* beached exactly where it is today![32]

Albert Hill. When the people came back [to York Factory] after
winter trapping, after the river breaks up,[33] sometimes they
wouldn't use their canoes. They used rafts. They would drift towards York Factory. The Hudson's Bay Company used to buy
timbers. So the people would build rafts and sell the timbers
when they got to York Factory. The rafts were about the size of
this area.[34] To build your raft you would stop along the way
down-river and pick out the big trees. You pick a good spot
where there are a lot of good trees and make camp. You always
had enough trees to make the original raft larger. The company
bought wood at any time.
Amy Hill. Yes, the company bought the wood because that's all it
used for heating the buildings.
Albert Hill. If you were going to travel at night on the raft you
built a wigwam on it! But you only travel at night if the river is
calm.
Amy Hill. You slept inside the wigwam.
Albert Hill. If it was too windy you didn't travel on the raft at
night. You went to shore and made camp. You pull the raft on
shore and secure it so it doesn't get damaged during the night
from the wind and water.
Amy Hill. We made a raft but it was our own. The Hudson's Bay
Company didn't buy wood then. Anyway, my daughter Nora
was just a baby then and there was her older sister. We drifted
down the river during the night. The children and I slept in the
wigwam. The children were tied up so they wouldn't stray to the
edge of the raft!

Fred Beardy. The food we ate while travelling was what was
killed during this time. We had tea and a little flour but we

Dragging a York boat across a portage on the Hayes River, n.d. (Provincial Archives of Manitoba).

survived on the game that was killed. At that time, everyone was raised in this way and we survived. From there [the trapline] we came by canoe, using paddles, and there would still be some ice on the river. At times we would push the ice or go around it. We usually travelled when it was high tide and we'd travel close to shore. After this they started using the two-masted boats but the river had to be almost clear of ice for these boats. They used these for a long time. They were still using these two-masted boats when you [Flora Beardy] were born. It was hard travelling with these, especially if there was a lot of ice. They would have to use long poles to move the boat along and it would take a long time. In one tide, sometimes the boat would only advance one mile! These boats were used for quite some time.[35]

Abel Chapman. They didn't use dogs at that time. That's how people travelled a long time ago – they walked. It's just lately that dogs were used for travel. Everybody travelled by walking, even children.

COMPANY AND COMMUNITY

John Neepin. These white men that lived there [York Factory] used to treat the Indians good. That's what I was told. If one of the white men killed a moose, he shared it with the Indians and didn't expect anything in return, so the Indians treated him the same.

This was the way of the Hudson's Bay Company, according to stories that were told. The company fed the people when they were at York Factory during the summer. They fed everyone. Even the ones that got wood for the company. They were also given food. Even though the company knew they had credit left from their earnings during the winter, they gave them food. The story was that people found all sorts of ways to earn their keep. The company also helped. Take for instance the old men. They were given rope to take apart [to make oakum]. This was usually used for stuffing and filling cracks. They earned money for doing this and other odd jobs. So when the people left for the winter they usually had some credit in the store. They would buy their groceries and leave for trapping.[36]

Interior of York Factory store, 1910. (Provincial Archives of Manitoba,
A.V. Thomas Collection, 98).

Joseph Saunders. We didn't come to York Factory until Christmas. I went to pay my bill and noticed that the old man [HBC clerk] had added our pay for unloading the Schooner onto our bill [instead of subtracting it from what was owed]! He didn't think we'd find out but we did. He must have kept the money and then added it to our account! Anyway, we didn't pay the difference. That's how crooked he was. We called him *Kihci-pôcôw.*[37] I guess he was a clerk at a lot of other places and nobody liked him because they knew he was crooked and could not be trusted. They found out how he was treating the people. Anyway, when he left York Factory, it was us that took him by boat. It was a hot, hot, sunny day when we left York Factory. Not a day for paddling! When we came around Marsh Point we decided to stop because it was too hot. So we all went ashore and decided to wait for the evening tide. The place where we stopped was called "high banks." The minister [Richard Faries] was also with us. He was escorting some children who were going out to school. And this clerk, Mr *Pôcôw,* wouldn't sit with us. He sat off by himself. He was sitting on a rock with his head hanging down.

Richard Beardy. This one time the big boss got mad, the Hudson's Bay Company boss.[38] He didn't want to give out any more food to the men. The ship captain was always in a hurry. He came in so the men had to work hard and fast! He was every time always in a hurry. Anyway, my father, who was the chief then,[39] told the boss of the Hudson's Bay Company, "If you're not going to give out any food, these men are not going to work!" I think this was the first strike at York Factory! The men wouldn't work if they weren't going to get paid. I think it's written down somewhere about the strike. The boss got real mad and said, "All of you get off the Hudson's Bay Company property!" My father told the men: "Go home! Get off this property! If they don't want to pay us, we won't work!" So they all followed my dad, even the half-breeds! Meanwhile the boat is sitting out there with all the cargo and nobody to unload it. The big boss wasn't too pleased about that. Anyway, he finally gave in and informed the men he would give out food. All the men went back to work and started unloading the boat. He, the big boss, was just trying to get work done without paying the men!

Eliza Oman ("*Kihci* Cook") at York Factory, *c.* 1930s. (Courtesy of John Ingram).

Chief Abraham Beardy and wife Sally, n.d. (Courtesy of Flora Beardy).

Albert Hill. A person got quite a bit of money for what is known as a cord of wood. A cord was usually ... let's see ... two feet and two feet ... it was eight feet long. And it was four feet high. Sometimes you cut four of these cords and sell them. The company bought these and from the money you received you were able to purchase lots of food.

Amy Hill. You didn't receive any money, but the wood was like money. It went on your credit.

[The HBC clerks] we knew were friendly. They knew how to flirt with the women! The reason why I'm saying this is one of the women, Christina, used to call them her boyfriends! The clerks were called "the ones with the white caps." She would say they were her boyfriends! That's why I said this. They used to flirt! Yes, they were friendly. I've heard other people say this. They didn't dislike the Indians.

Albert Hill. Yes, they were friendly with the Indians. Some were proud of the Indians, especially the elders. Lots of respect for the elders.

Alex Ouscan. I don't know how the company counted this [payment for goods or labour], but everything was paid by skins. You can buy so many things for a certain amount of pelts. Same thing when a person worked for the company: their pay or money amount was in fur value.[40]

Archelaus Beardy. The job I had was to go and get the mail. I eventually got these duties. I went to Gillam. This is where we used to go and pick up the mail. I think it was about three years that I had this job. We also carried mailbags, letters to women from the clerks that worked at Gillam.

Abel Chapman. There was also this guy they called *Paskwastik-wân*.[41] This was where he sold his goods. They didn't go and sell where the Hudson's Bay Company store was. And at Wanatawahak this person's name was Mr Ray.[42] He was a trader there for quite some time. Then after Mr Ray left another trader came there. I can't remember this one's name. Then later on Joe Chambers arrived there. He came there and sold his goods for some time. While he was trading, he also trapped near the area. Then the

Men from York Factory, *c.* 1930s. *Left to right:* Joe Spence, Andrew Lavallee, unidentified, unidentified, Bill McDonald, Daniel Spence, Thomas Redhead, Hamilton Gibeault, James McPherson, Josiah Beardy, and Fred McPherson. (Courtesy of Barbara Gordon).

very last trader that came there was Andrew Lavallee. And the man they called Luke.[43] That was the last of the traders. The only one left was the Hudson's Bay Company.

This grandfather of mine, while he was the chief,[44] he would gather the people together, the ones that arrived in late spring after the rivers open. There would be usually two men to come and see him, two great men, leaders of the people. Each would give two special pelts and also one of all other pelts. These were given to my grandfather when they arrived there at this time of year. Then he would go and sell them to the Hudson's Bay Company. He would go and sell these pelts. He would put all the other furs together and sell them. Then what he received would go towards their credit and the rest is left on their account. He, my grandfather, had his own money account. He never drank up his money! That money that he looked after in the accounts was for everybody, for all his people so when a family ran short of food, money was taken from this account and food was purchased for them. If they were desperate and had no food at all, he would get them food. He would get the councillors to go and give the family this food. This was always available, and also if there was to be a wedding, money was taken for food. Food was donated towards the feast. The amount of food that was needed was calculated and the Hudson's Bay Company always went half with my grandfather. My grandfather half and the Company half.

RECREATION AND SOCIAL EVENTS

Fred Beardy. [The Shamattawa people] would come to York Factory. Boy, there used to be a lot of people at York Factory during the summer. The old-timers then knew how to play music. These fellows from Shamattawa could play: Sammy Beardy, Roderick Redhead, and William, William Redhead, and Sanders Redhead. These guys could really play the violin!

There were lots of weddings. Sometimes at one wedding there would be ten couples getting married.[45] Oh yes, they would dress up. The men wore suits and hats, straw hats. [The women] sewed their own dresses. They also wore shawls.

Well they would have the games on July 1st. All sorts of games.

Group wedding at the Church of St John of York Factory, 2 August 1926. *Left to right:* Alex Hill and Eliza Redhead, Albert Hill and Amy Redhead, Stephen Beardy and Christine Cooper, and William Beardy and Jennie Chapman. (Courtesy of Albert and Amy Hill).

Tug of war, the ladies did this and the men too. Another fun game was when a person puts a sack on their legs. This was the hardest one! The other one was where two people tie their ankles together. You have to hold each other while you're running! Another one was back packing. The person would try and pack as much as they can. A lot of people used to enter this one. Boy, some people would pack a lot of weight! We also had relay races. This one guy, Sanders Redhead, used to win this all the time but he eventually got beat! We had these races on the football field. The posts were far apart and the judges would put a piece of paper on each end of the field between the posts. The guys running would start from opposite ends, pick up the paper, run it back to where they started, and pass it on to the next fellow. And boy would they run! Simeon was a fast runner, the late Simeon Spence. He won the race that day. He beat everybody, even Sanders Redhead!

We played football.[46] The guys from Shamattawa would be on one end and the York Factory guys on the other. The Shamattawa team never beat the York Factory team! We would beat them every game! We played football a lot at that time.

Mary Redhead. They used to play football [at York Factory]. I remember seeing the men play football, some of the ones who lived up-river. Right up-river. There was a clearing there right up to the last house. This was where they played. Sarah and Simeon Spence used to have a house in that area. We used to go and visit there.[47]

There were lots of good dancers. When I first started dancing I used to like doing the jig. At one dance, I was jigging and nobody would take over for me! I had already beaten five men and nobody would take over! That's when I knew that I was a good dancer, especially jigging.

Oh yes! If there were others just arriving, they'd start all over again! Sometimes they had three dances in one night! Oh, the people loved dancing. Every chance they had they would have a dance. The elders too! They were the ones who usually held dances.

Elizabeth Oman. At Christmas the minister use to put up a Christmas tree. At school, in the school. He used to hang all kinds of

Wedding group at York Factory, *c*. 1930s. *Front row, left to right:*
Amelia Saunders, Jeremiah Stoney, and Rebecca Stoney. (Courtesy
of John Ingram).

toys on the tree with our names on it! Little dolls, things like that. [At Christmas] the Indians would all arrive there [at York Factory] at that time. All the kids used to have new moccasins. When Christmas time comes everybody's happy!

Archelaus Beardy. At Christmas we moved away from there, to York Factory. We'd go there just before Christmas and come back to Wanatawahak after New Year's Day or "Kissing Day."[48] Then we would go to York Factory again at Easter. We went to York Factory quite often. Mainly to go to the store. They had dances. They had dances at the house of the boss. This was the big boss's house. His name was Mr Hardy.[49] Yes, this is where they held the dances, where he lived. They would block off a certain area for the dance. The Hudson's Bay Company also gave out food during Christmas. Then there would be a feast.

David Massan. On New Year's Eve people would travel from house to house, using dog teams, right until midnight! During this time the church bell would be ringing and there would be shooting! The guns would be fired into the air. People would be driving around with their dog teams. The next morning the people would go around from house to house shaking hands with everyone. To all the houses. They used to have this big thing, some kind of instrument, like a big horn. It was pointed on one end and it was pretty long. I don't know what it was called. Anyway when you pull it from one end it would make a big noise! Like a loud tooting sound. That's how it sounds. People carried this around and if you keep pulling on it, it makes a loud noise. They also had good times and games on New Year's Day. That's what this one councillor said. Thomas was his name. He said it was fun on New Year's Day because they played soccer/football. Especially when the women played. He said it was very exciting to watch. Like heaven!

Richard Beardy. When one couple got married they had their maid of honour and the best man. One man and one woman. Then the rest of the party consisted of sometimes eight women and their partners.[50] Then they would all walk in a line to the church! It used to look so nice. Sometimes there would be four

Playing cards at York Factory, c. 1940. *Left to right:* Archelaus Beardy, Stephen
Taylor, Willy Gray, and Solomon Hill. (Courtesy of John Ingram).

couples getting married! You should have seen this long line of people.[51] The area they would leave from was nice. It was all clearing, no trees. Anyway the church was quite a ways especially from Mr Faries's house.[52] But they all walked the distance. The wedding party would leave from near where George Spence used to live, a long way from the church. There also used to be a yellow building there, and Sammy Gray's house. That's where they left from. There was a long line of people. Behind these people there was usually someone playing music. Most of the time it was my dad and he would be playing the "instrument that you stretch," the accordion.

Joseph Saunders. This was the main type of recreation, football and dancing. The people from Shamattawa were the best dancers at that time. We used to challenge each other.

FOOD, CLOTHING, AND SHELTER

Amelia Saunders. Oh, we ate a lot of berries! These were always part of the diet, like meat. Soon as the berries were ready we would all get together and pick them.[53]
Joseph Saunders. You know the ptarmigans, the big, white ones? Well you never throw the intestines away. Part of the intestine was eaten![54]
Amelia Saunders. On the rabbit, nothing was wasted. We just throw the feet away. The rest was eaten – nothing was wasted then.
Joseph Saunders. Just like the geese, all the feet were dried and put away. Sometime, in the future, they would be boiled and eaten. These made for one meal. All food tasted good if it was prepared properly. All geese would be smoked or dried. You can do this to anything!

Alex Ouscan. A long time ago people ate polar bear. They didn't throw away the meat. They'd eat the whole bear. They would dry the meat and render down the fat for oil.[55] As was done with caribou meat, any meat, fat, or rendered oil was stuffed and carried in the caribou stomach. The stomach was properly cleaned before it was used.

Archelaus Beardy. I ate polar bear meat once. I just thought I'd try some. My father had killed a polar bear. He rinsed off the meat and put it in a grinder with some salt pork/bacon, made patties, and fried it. It looked good while it was cooking, so when it was done I started eating it. At first it didn't taste too bad. After about three bites it sure tasted awful! I didn't dare eat anymore. My father used to tell me that polar bear paws tasted good. He used to say that the paws tasted almost like moose nose!

Joseph Saunders. Oh, there were lots of whales. We were allowed to kill them and use them for dog food. Some people who ate the whales would only eat the whale fat. Some people said after rendering the fat they would eat the refuse that was left. These were the people that lived at the portage. This is where they caught the whales. He used to tell us that they would eat some while the whale was fresh. He said it tasted pretty good! This was where they rendered the fat and prepared food for the dogs.[56]

Another thing I remember, a long time ago, when we were living at Kaskatamagun, was this. During the winter, we would leave and go inland, looking for caribou. The caribou don't stay along the coast during the winter; they go inland. Then that's when we would move inland. All we would take is some fish. Some were cooked and some were raw but frozen. This was our food. When we made camp we would just chop off the skin and boil the fish. Then we would drink the broth. This was our tea!

During the time we spent away from York Factory, we would be out trapping and hunting caribou. If we killed a lot, not one bit of food was wasted. We would render grease and make pemmican. The meat always tasted good, if prepared properly. The same with the geese. Not a thing wasted, a long time ago. Everything was eaten.

John Neepin. Today, I think, the cause of all these different sicknesses that we have today is from all the different foods that people eat. So many things in the foods. After I moved to the railroad, while I worked on the railroad, I lots of times felt like I hadn't eaten, although I had eaten the food everyone else was eating! Potatoes and the white man's meat. Just like I wasn't eating meat at all! I would be hungry in no time. Well, I guess, that's how it is. If you're use to eating wild food and you haven't had any for some time, you are always hungry! Even after you've eaten something else. Then a person who eats the white man's food, all the time, is not like that. This food satisfies him. I know this, because I used to be so hungry all the time after eating the white man's food. This was how I was, at first. I always craved the food that I was used to eating. I needed to have some wild food. We weren't able to get wild food. The white man would stop us from hunting our own food. I should have never let them stop us from hunting our own food. They weren't being fair to us. They made us eat their food and stopped us from eating ours.

David Massan. Wanatoyak are pretty hard.[57] You can knock them off the tree. They're brown/yellow in the middle and dry. When you burn this it takes a long time before it burns out. You would get a big piece and put it inside a pail. Then you would cover the pail. Meanwhile this thing is burning or smoldering all the time it's being carried around. It won't burn out for a long time. That's what they used to do. They carried their stove around with them! And when you want to make a fire, you just blow on this to start one. You just put another one in the pail before the first one is completely burnt up.

Once I saw a person completely make a canoe, a birchbark canoe. They would lay the birch out on the ground and then sew them together with tree roots. It's easy to sew the birch with these roots. Then after they finished sewing the bark together, it was ready to put on the canoe frame. The frame is made from tamarack. These tamarack strips are shaped and bent and narrowed down as you reach the front and back of the canoe. They would bend the tamarack strip and tie it into place and leave it until it dries. When it dried you had the formed shape of that part of canoe. These tamarack strips were planed to size using a crooked knife, larger in the centre and narrower to the front and back. Then they would clear off the smooth surface and spread the birch strips that had been sewn together, on it. They put two supports on each end where the canoe frame is placed. The birch coverings are laid beside the canoe frame, neatly spread out. When a strip is placed down the frame, rocks are used to hold it in place. Then gradually all the strips are sewn together over the frame.

Then the birch is pulled tightly over the frame and tucked in on the inside of the canoe.

They sew the birch strips as they worked, eventually covering the back and nose part of the canoe, the front. They did a good job and all they used for sewing the strips together was tree roots. Then they made two reinforcements. These boards [thwarts] would be placed about four feet apart. Not right in the centre but more towards the end and front. These are fastened to the canoe frame by tree roots. Holes were made in the boards so they could thread the roots into them. That made the birchbark canoe just about complete. All this was done with no nails, not even one nail.

After this was done then the canoe was turned upside down. This was when the gum, from the [spruce] trees, was used. This was spread on the parts that were sewn together. The tree gum was collected and melted down and spread on the sewn areas. After this was done then the canoe was put in the upright position. After the gum dried then water was poured into the canoe. This was to see if there were any leaks. If it leaked, that spot was marked with a piece of charred wood. When this was done and there no more leaks, then the canoe was painted. This fellow painted his canoe red! He used the red willow. This willow, when put in water, turns the water red. He painted the canoe with it. The canoe was bright red! After this he was all finished. The birchbark canoe was quite tough. It can hold a person plus some supplies and rarely capsized in rough water.[58]

A person couldn't get too much food. Just the bare necessities in the house. Flour, tea, and when you set out to travel you sometimes had very little of these and had to wait until summer to purchase more. It was usually the elder who looked after the tea. He conserved the tea by having tea only on Sundays. He would make it last just by having it on Sundays.

There was another way they made broth to drink. If a moose or caribou was killed, the bones were broken and boiled in a big pot. When this was done, all the grease or fat was then skimmed off and that left the broth to be drunk. This was very tasty and good for you. It was strained through a cloth so you don't get any of the bones. This was a common drink. Yes, the people saved their tea for Sundays.

[The children] would play with a small wooden boat in the water, pulling it along. It was made out of wood and it floated. This was the toy for the boys. They'd pull it along in the water and sometimes loaded it up with small rocks.

There was no clothing, like for instance, pants like these. There was nothing like that. They had this yellow brown strong cloth in the store [at Big Trout Lake]. This is what they used to make pants for the men, and also the women used this to make dresses. The other material they had was flannel/flannelette. This was thin material and was used mostly for underclothing for both men and women. For socks they had woollen ones but they weren't very long. They would come up to the knees. All the women wore these. I don't know what the women wore underneath, from the knees up, but it must have been cold for them! They used to work outside a lot and it was cold in the winter.

Abel Chapman. There weren't very many houses [at York Factory]. People lived in tents. The tents were put up all over the area. I remember seeing not too many, the ones they called wigwams. Not too many, but I remember seeing some, while people still used them. I remember seeing smoke coming out of them. Wigwams, the ones you see sometimes on TV. People started building cabins. As time went on there were more and more houses. The people would get big trees and they would saw the trees into planks to build the wooden houses. They would raft them [the trees or planks] down from up the river. Then later on the company brought in wooden planks by schooner, and also nails and roofing paper. With all this available there were lots of houses built. This wasn't too long before the people left there.

Powder was used for these [old] guns. The powder would be put in, then the wad, and then the bullet. They worked hard using these guns. All this was pushed down. Sometimes the gun had two barrels and sometimes just one. Yes, my father used to talk about these guns. They had round bullets. He said in one winter he killed thirty caribou, using this type of gun. He would put the round bullet in his mouth before he loaded it into the gun, so it will not roll out. That's why he did this. If he didn't wet it, the bullet will roll out of the gun barrel. After these guns, my father said, came the ones called .44s. Our grandfathers didn't like these very much! They were called .44s. The bullets were like rifle bullets. The bullet travelled quite far. This was the first time we saw rifles. Then today there are new guns.

Alex Ouscan. [My mother] said they made wigwams out of caribou skins. The skins were sewn together, after the hair had been removed from them, and softened. They were sewn together and placed around the poles. That was their covering. The hides weren't tanned. They were used raw and sewn together.[59]

WOMEN'S LIVES AND ACTIVITIES

David Massan. Women did lots of work. Skinning. They skinned the animals and dried the pelts. That was their job. And looking after the children. [The children] would just play, I guess. Some of the older ones would probably cut firewood.
Mary Redhead. The women didn't mind working in those days. There wasn't anything hard about it. No hesitating. It was something that was done daily. No, the women never complained. Strange, aye? That's how it was.

Amelia Saunders. We even used to hunt for caribou too. We hunted a lot, just like the men. We were taught this as we were growing up.
Joseph Saunders. They had guns and hunted with them. They would shoot ptarmigans. Some of the women were pretty good shots, especially shooting geese!

Catherine Anderson. One time, this old lady[60] and I killed one moose each! She wasn't that old. When you hear a person say *nôcikwêsiw* it means old woman. But this woman wasn't that old – she was fairly young. She killed a moose. This was in the summer and I shot mine early spring. I got a female moose but she wasn't carrying any young. She was fat! We also used to hunt moose in the fall. Just before mating season. This woman was a pretty fast runner. If we saw moose tracks we would follow them. If we knew we were getting close then we would look for some

Unidentified woman and child at York Factory, 1930s. (Courtesy of John Ingram).

tall trees and climb them, taking our guns along. If the moose was close enough we would shoot from the tree! Then we'd dry the meat. When I took the hair off the hide I would use a knife. I didn't have the bone that's usually used to cut off the hair. Then after the hair is cut off, the hide is fleshed and soaked. Then it is rubbed with the brain of the animal. This softens the hide. Then it is hung to dry.[61]

Albert Hill. When we arrived here at Gillam, it was here that Nora Jean [Massan] killed a caribou.
Amy Hill. She was just like a man!
Albert Hill. Yes, she did things a man would normally do. This fellow, his name was Simeon, this was her older brother. He's the one that taught her how to hunt. I guess one day she expressed to her brother how she wished for the caribou that were nearby. Her brother then asked her: "Why do you wish for them? Why do you just look at them? Did you not know that you can kill a caribou with a .22 gun?" Well, Nora Jean did not know this. She thought the bullet was too small to kill a caribou. Anyway he showed her how to use the gun, and from then on she always hunted caribou and was able to kill them!

Amy Hill. I was in the hospital when I had one of my children. I had five altogether. The youngest one, Abner, was born in The Pas hospital. We were living in Shamattawa but they had to fly me to The Pas. At Shamattawa, this big chunk of ice had washed up on the riverbank and I went to collect some. He [her husband, Albert] had gone up-river by canoe to check his traps. He wasn't home at the time. I was pregnant with Abner then. Anyway I chopped the ice and filled up my bag. As I swung the bag onto my back I felt a very sharp pain! I fell down – that's how bad the pain was. I was suffering so much they called for a plane and flew me to The Pas. The doctor found that somehow the baby had shifted from the normal position. They managed to move the baby back to the proper position again. The baby survived and so did I.

Flora Beardy. I remember my brothers had bows and arrows. My mother and granny always told me not to play with them. They said if I played with them my breasts would grow until they dragged on the ground!

Mary Redhead. With me, before I got married, I was told that whenever I went to visit at Billy's[62] house, on my way I was to pick some spruce boughs or willows, and sit on these wherever I sat while I was in his house! This was showing respect for the man.

John Neepin. The women carried water, chopped wood, and also went and got the wood. They'd carry the wood on their back. That's what the women did. In the winter they'd haul snow and melt it for water. The woman didn't waste any time. She was alway working, doing things around the house, inside and outside. She didn't have appliances where she just turns a knob, like the stove. The cooking area was made of mud. The mud would be piled and the fire lit in the centre. The pot that is to boil would be hung on a pole over the fire.

Mary Redhead. Yes. You put the child in the cradle, stand it up, and do whatever work you're doing. It worked for us! The child is safely in the cradle.[63] We'd go and gather wood or chop some.

Abel Chapman. A long time ago when the girls were young they were told how to prepare themselves for childbirth. They were told to always stay active, especially for their first pregnancy. If they were active during their pregnancy then their labour would be easier. Not to stay in bed too long. To get up early. The ones that suffered didn't listen to this. They did not stay active. Sometimes the child died inside the mother. Some young mothers did not listen, just like today. A lot of them are not active enough. Being active made the childbirth easier. There weren't very many children lost in childbirth.

Nobody used diapers. Moss, that's what was used. The women worked hard. They gathered the moss in the summer and hung it to dry, before the moss started to freeze. If a woman knew she was going to have her baby before the following summer, she would pick the moss during the previous summer and dry it. She knew when she would have her baby so she prepared the moss ahead of time. This is what was used.

York Factory group, *c. 1950. Back row, left to right:* Elizabeth Ouscan, Mary Spence, Mary Ann McPherson, Alice Ouscan, and Eliza Spence. *Front row:* Flora Beardy, Dinah Dick, and Simeon Spence. (Courtesy of Flora Beardy).

A woman, at that time, worked just as hard as a man. They, too, hunted. They took good care of him. They snared rabbits and also set nets for fish.

GROWING UP AT YORK FACTORY

David Massan. Work started early. After everyone ate, the work started. We had to get water and cut firewood. If there were rabbit snares to be checked, the children did that. Check the snares. When all this was done, the children were allowed to play. Then late afternoon they were called to do more work. Sometimes they were sent a long way to get something to eat. That's what they did. They worked most of the time.

Catherine Anderson. [When the ship arrived] people used to steal things and hide them! There was a place nearby where they unloaded the boats, and that's where they would hide these things. Us kids used to watch them. We used to find canned goods and then we would move them to the bush! Close to where the cow and horse stable was. That's where we used to move the stuff to. There would be whole slabs of salt pork, sometimes. The slabs were sometimes dirty but if they were cleaned you could eat it. We used to see these guys hide their stuff and then we would go and move them. One time we saw Willy Gray while we were in the bush and called him. He was standing there looking around. We got scared so we didn't call him again. The things we found. We took them to the store and we would get paid for it!

At ship time we wouldn't go home. We would hang around the boathouse. Sometimes we would ask for some things and they would give it to us. We would go see this woman they called *Kihci* [Big] Cook.[64] She used to feed us. So we wouldn't go home for lunch. We would eat at the kitchen. Yes, we used to find lots of things [hidden by those unloading the boat]. Sugar in ten-pound packages. They were about this size. We used to find lots of these. The boss would pay us good because we helped him get the goods back!

We would use parts of branches for dolls. We would shape the head and the shoulders and make eyes. These were our toys. They were made out of wood.

Children with cannon near the riverbank, September 1916. (Provincial Archives of Manitoba, John Campbell Collection, 143).

Mary Redhead. They used to have horses at York Factory, you know. One time we were walking down-river and we met these horses! Oh hie! They were standing right in the middle of the trail and wouldn't move. They were moving their heads and their ears. We were so scared! We walked on the shore to get around them!

People used to tease me, telling me that Billy [Redhead] was going to be my husband! I'd say: "Let him marry someone else! I don't want him for a husband!" We used to laugh about this a lot because I ended up marrying him!

Abel Chapman. The only toys the children played with were usually carved out of wood. Out of wooden stumps. Then they would stand them up away from them. Do you know what I mean? They line up the carved wooden stumps on one end. The game where they roll a ball at these things. They knock all the wooden sticks down. [Bowling] that's the one! That's how the children would line up the sticks. Then they try and knock them all down.

These dolls were made by the girls and the grandmothers would make clothes for them. They used cotton to make the clothes so the girls could play with them. The girls liked playing with these homemade dolls.

That's what all the children did mostly. The young boys would play football and they all liked dancing. Sometimes dancing went on all night without a single glass of alcohol.

The year 1947. This was the year of "Being Born" or "The Birth" on the 10th of February. The birth of my daughter. The one that lost her life in the fire at Gillam. We had just the two children, at that time.[65] Helen [was her name]. John James [Massan] was her husband. Yes, I never forget her.

CHURCHES AND MINISTERS

Richard Beardy. This religion we have today,[66] [York Factory] is where it came from. This white man's religion was brought to York Factory. Then it was taken to the other side of this big body of water.[67] Then this religion was met halfway with another

The Church of St John of York Factory, 1916. Built under the direction of HBC Chief Factor James Hargrave in 1858, this church was torn down in 1934 and replaced by a new building at the Anglican Mission property up-river. (Provincial Archives of Manitoba, John Campbell Collection, 164).

religion, the Indian religion. This is what we have today. A bit of both. They say this happened maybe 200 years ago.

Joseph Saunders. One of the churches [at York Factory] was called the English church.[68]
Amelia Saunders. This was the tin church.[69]
Joseph Saunders. Yes, and the other one was the Cree church. When this church got old they built another one, farther up the river. That was a pretty big church too, the one that rotted away. The Hudson's Bay Company built that church, the one that was down-river. They built it for the Indians.[70] As for the church that was up the river, the Indians all pitched in to help pay for this building.[71] They donated fur pelts. These pelts were given to the minister. Yes, but we would also go to the minister's house at any time and give him furs, and then he would sell them to the Hudson's Bay Company. This is how we got the money to buy materials needed to build the church. Offering in the church was separate.

Fred Beardy. Archdeacon Faries. I think he was at York Factory for forty-eight years before he left. He lived there for a long time.[72] He used to travel all over. He would go from York Factory to Sturgeon River. He would use a canoe and paddle, no motor. He would also take a rope because sometimes they would have to drag the canoe. He would make it to Sturgeon River okay. They had to make lots of portages.

Mrs Faries always played the music. She knew how. She really knew how to play the organ. That's when I learnt how to play the organ. I must have been about sixteen years old when I started working in the church. I would help the minister and I would play the organ in church.

Albert Hill. Well, people use to say that the minister [Mr Faries] was alone when he came to York Factory. He wasn't married yet. There was this one old man who used to joke with him about this. He would say to Mr Faries: "Well, at least you're not living by yourself. You have a cat!" He would go on and ask him, "No woman yet?" To which Mr Faries would reply, "No. No woman yet!" It wasn't too long after this that he got married.

The Reverend Richard and Catherine Faries, n.d. (Courtesy of Flora Beardy).

Amy Hill. His wife wasn't too kind. She was mean! The reason I say this is because she was mean to us. When I was at York Factory my friends and I would go pick berries in this one area. It was a clearing and it wasn't that close to her house. Anyway as soon as she'd see us there she'd come running towards us waving her stick! We were afraid of her so we'd run away.

Elizabeth Oman. In the morning, old Faries held a service in the English church and in the afternoon and evening [at the big church] twice. The minister held three services each Sunday. A service was held in the morning in the English church and in the other one, the one that was called the big church, three o'clock in the afternoon and sometimes seven o'clock in the evening. That's when services were. And every Wednesday a service was held in the evening.

Mary Redhead. The small church.[73] That church was nice. As far as I can remember we used to go to church there and it was in good condition.

The story is that [Mr Faries] lived at York Factory for many years. When he died they found him sitting in his chair, holding his Bible in his lap. He had been dead for some time before he was found.

Catherine Anderson. I had all my children baptized at York Factory whenever we returned from the trapline. We would travel to York Factory from where we were trapping. My one boy didn't get baptized until late spring and he was born in early winter. One other time I had to get my daughter baptized, when we arrived at York Factory. I saw your [Flora Beardy's] mother so I asked her to be a godparent for my daughter. She agreed to be her godmother.

Archelaus Beardy. The people gave offering once. No, three times a year. I never ever heard the minister say that there wasn't enough money for the church. On Christmas Day, Easter Sunday and during the summer. In July. When I go to church [today] I find that the church is almost empty. Just a few people here and there. At York Factory it was different. The big church would just

Local people in front of the "iron" church, n.d. Richard and Catherine Faries are standing centre. (Courtesy of Flora Beardy).

be packed. People would be standing outside because there would be no more room inside. Another thing was the way people dressed when they went to church. They didn't wear just any old clothes; the men wore suits and neckties. They dressed and looked very nice.

Abel Chapman. If I knew how to speak English I would tell these people who make laws a few things. I read the Bible a lot. God is the one that provided everything on this earth. Laws, everything that we use in order to survive. Today, the white man wants to stamp out God's laws and make his own. He thinks his laws are higher or more important than the Creator's. It is written, after the Creator completed the work, that the creatures on this earth are to be used by all the people. To be used when needed so the people can live. All these animals and the birds that fly. That we hunt these and live off them. This was promised to us. The white man was also promised them. To have gardens and eat what it bears, to live off them. To live off the gardens. He was promised other things that lived and grew in their areas. Now the white man has gone above these laws the Creator made. He wants to control everything. Even our hunting. So I often think someday they [white men] will see the wrong they have done, their mistakes. This is not right, to go against the Creator.

He [Mr Faries] was a minister at York Factory for fifty-three years. He travelled from place to place, using a dog team. He never used a plane. In the summer he would go to Fort Severn and he would use a boat. Of all the ministers I know of he was the only one that travelled so much by boat and dog team. I think of all the married couples at York Factory, Mr Faries performed all the services. The children also. Most, if not all of them, were probably baptized by Mr Faries. Yes, that minister did all this. After him there was another minister, not too long before we left York Factory.[74] Mr Faries was the minister that was there all these years, doing baptisms, church services, and weddings.

EDUCATION

Amelia Saunders. When the time came for our children to go to school, that's when we moved to York Factory, for good, from

Kaskatamagun. After that, just Joseph would go hunt and trap at
Kaskatamagun. Some of our kids were brought out of York Factory to go to school. We didn't allow the oldest girl, Dorothy, to
leave. That's the only one we kept. We let the other ones leave
to go to school.

Archelaus Beardy. There's a funny story about this old school [at
York Factory].[75] Mr Faries owned a bull at York Factory. This bull
was young and he was wicked. I was told that one day, while the
kids were in school, the bull charged the door of the schoolhouse
and managed to push it open! I guess there was a shovel standing by the door so the teacher used this to hit the bull. He was
trying to drive it back outside! Finally the teacher drove the bull
outside. While he was outside I guess the bull charged him and
knocked him to the ground! I guess the teacher was lying there
flat on his back. He was lucky he didn't get gored because the
bull had horns.

Albert Hill. I never went to school.
Amy Hill. When we did go to school the teacher spent his time
learning Cree! He was a white man. He was a young guy.

Catherine Anderson. One time we were told that there was going
to be a new teacher the next day. This guy that came to our house
said that not only one teacher came in but that there were two
of them! The next morning we all ran to the church. We were all
excited! We wanted to see the new teachers. Then we saw two
people coming. This was just before the service started. The guys
that were coming were your [Flora Beardy's] uncle Frederick and
your grandfather Jimmy Inkster. They were the ones everyone
was talking about. Hamilton [Gibeault] was standing beside me,
at that time, and he was laughing![76]

Elizabeth Oman. McKay school is the first school I went to. In The
Pas, that's where McKay school was.[77] The McKay school burnt
so then we were sent to Elkhorn.[78] The year 1940 was when I
came home from Elkhorn.
Flora Beardy. Oh! So you were away for seven years?
Elizabeth Oman. Yes!

McKay Residential School at The Pas, *c.* 1923. (Provincial Archives of Manitoba, Malaher Collection, 3).

Flora Beardy. You didn't even come home for the summer?
Elizabeth Oman. No.

Mary Redhead. [We were sent] to the school that was in The Pas. It was called McKay School. That's where we were sent. There were two that didn't come back to where we were going to school. There were three ... Let's see, at the beginning there were five of us that left York Factory. Three girls and two boys.
Flora Beardy. You also said you went to Elkhorn school.
Mary Redhead. Yes, that's another place they sent us. All five of us. The ones I just named. We came by train and then I went back to York Factory by canoe. I went by boat. My grandfather Peter Massan used to travel between here and York Factory. That's who I went with. Rebecca[79] was a young girl also at that time. By the time we got to York Factory my grandfather was angry with us. Every time we camped he'd lose us! We'd run up the riverbank and go pick berries. We weren't worried about lunch. He would make camp and have tea. He would call for us saying if we didn't come right away he would leave without us! We didn't want to leave the berries. We'd grab an extra handful and then run back to the canoe.

That was the beginning of sending children away from York Factory for schooling. At that time, the children never came home. Not like now, they come home for the summer. Nobody came home until they completed their full education. As far as I can remember we never came home. We stayed at the school all year. Some of the students who lived in towns close to the school were allowed to go home but we weren't. They said York Factory was too far. We would have to go by plane and it was too expensive. We went hungry lots of times. They didn't feed us enough so lots of times we were hungry. At the school we were only allowed one slice of bread. This woman used to give us extra bread to eat but we had to hide it! I don't understand why they treated us like that. When we worked we worked at different jobs. We also went to clean houses. We stayed on one job for one week.
Flora Beardy. Were you and the rest ever lonesome for home?
Mary Redhead. Holy smokes! Don't even ask that. I was in the hospital for a month when my father died. I was in there for one

month! The doctor thought I was going to die. I almost died
from grief and loneliness.

SICKNESS AND MEDICAL CARE

David Massan. This sickness came from a faraway place off to
the east.[80] I don't know how to say it in English. Where the
Ocicâhkosak[81] live. My uncle used to go there while he was trapping [with his partner]. When they got to this settlement everyone was sick, they were so sick that the people couldn't do
anything for themselves. They started cutting wood for everyone
who couldn't help themselves. They did this and headed back
for Trout River. They didn't want to stay too long. They were
both fine and well when they got back. This was the beginning of
spring. About a week later there were some people who started
getting sick. Also, at this time there were quite a few people
living in one house. The epidemic spread quickly. People were
dying. If a person got a bit of a chill then they would go into an
epileptic seizure, as well as having a fever. There was no medicine available then. The people would just lie on the floor. Some
people had no chairs or beds. When the door was opened you
could feel the cold draft. Lots of people were dying, sometimes
four in one day. Mostly the elders and middle-aged people. Some
babies also, not too many. People die in pairs/couples. Sometimes one by one. The cemetery got larger and covered this huge
clearing. That's how many people died. There were lots of people
there but not too many left after this illness.

Fred Beardy. A long time ago the minister was the doctor. It's just
lately that a doctor would come to York Factory. He would come
in the winter by plane. Sometimes he came twice in one winter.
He would only come once, during the winter, to Kaskatamagun.
This is just recently. The doctor's name was Dr Yule.[82] He flew
from place to place. This was when Lamb Airways was just starting. Tom Lamb and his plane.[83]

One time, there was a sickness called scarlet fever and a lot of
people got sick during this time. It was after this that the doctor
would come to York Factory more often. They had to bring all the

people out from Kaskatamagun. Everybody. The plane at times made two trips a day. They brought all the women and children out. Most of the men came by boat. Before this, there were a lot of people that died at York Factory. I think this was in 1926. I got sick too, at that time.

They used the Indian medicine men. These medicine men used herbs and other plants that grow on the land. I used these too. This one plant that grows all over, close to the ground, looks like spruce brush. Well, this was used to make a plaster. These were used a long time ago when someone got sick, especially if they were sick on any part of the body and if they were sick here [pointing to his chest]. I had a sore chest one time. I was sick for about three days. I had a hard time breathing. When you have this illness in the winter, snow can be used. The snow that's sitting right on top, not the snow on the bottom, the one on top, the snow that blows away. This is what my father used. You boil this snow water and drink it while it's steaming hot! Anyway this is what my father used and in no time I was well. This plaster was used and also *kâkikêpakwa*, a northern plant whose leaf is always green, the native tea plant.[84] This cured me one time.

One time, Jervois Spence and I were travelling together by dog team. This was in the winter and we were heading back to York Factory. Anyway, I was standing up in the back of my toboggan, going downhill to the lake, when all of a sudden something hit me! I didn't see this tree sticking out and it got me right here, right on the chest. I guess when I fell, I fell forward, right into the toboggan. We continued on, but my chest sure hurt. By that night I was coughing up blood. My father knew I was hurt bad so he made some *kâkikêpakwa*. Did it ever taste bitter! That's what I drank that night and you had to drink it while it was hot. By morning I felt a lot better. A lot of these herbs and plants that were used had medicine in them. A long time ago that's what these Indian medicine men used.

Elizabeth Oman. In the year 1927 there were a lot of people that died at that time. Many. There was a flu epidemic.[85]

Joseph Saunders. The minister was the one who looked after the medicine. We would just go and get him if someone was sick and he would minister to them. Especially the ones that were real sick from accidents with the guns. These guns weren't made the same as the guns we have today. Back then they used powder to fire the guns and the gun had a flintlock. When the guns were carried, sometimes the trigger lock would come undone, causing the gun to fire and usually wounding the carrier. Even when you bumped the gun it would shoot. My father had a gun like that.[86] Whenever he took it out he would use a double cover on the gun because he walked wherever he went and he knew that the gun wasn't too safe. One day while he was out hunting, it was a hilly area, he stopped to rest. He put the gun against a tree and the gun went off. It got him right here [pointing to his hand].

What I'm talking about happened a long time ago. Sometimes there would be a lot of sickness and a lot of people would die. But I don't know, I think it was in 1928 when they had the last sickness and a lot of people died in York Factory.[87] At that time we were living at Kaskatamagun but nobody got sick there. Not one person living at Kaskatamagun got sick. This was in 1923 and that was the first time we had a store here. This guy named Fred was the store manager then. But I had a brother-in-law named Frederick, who was at Kaskatamagun also. Fred was the first manager here; then Frederick became the manager later. This was the time when a lot of people died at York Factory. Anyway, Frederick went to York Factory and never came back. He got sick at York Factory and he died there. What happened was some people from Fort Severn passed by Kaskatamagun headed for York Factory, and Frederick tagged along with them. The store manager from Fort Severn had his wife on the boat. He was taking her to York Factory because she was sick and Frederick went along with them. He met up with the sickness that was at York Factory and died from it. Before this happened, my brother-in-law told me of the time his father and younger sister died at Fort Severn. This sister was older than my wife and her name was Sarah Jean. Sarah Jean was younger than your [Flora Beardy's] late granny Maryann.[88] Frederick said about his father's death: "When my father was sick, lying on the bed, I looked at him and just at that time he stopped breathing and when I turned around to go to my sister she also stopped breathing. They both died almost at the same time." My wife's family came to Kaskatamagun to tell her the news and took her back to Fort Severn for the funeral.

Archelaus Beardy. They never took anyone out of York Factory. It wasn't until just before I left York Factory that the plane would come in and fly out patients. The minister looked after the medicine. His name was Mr Faries. But a person couldn't get medicine whenever they wanted some because of Mrs Faries. She wasn't very nice. She would never let anyone into her house. She would open the door just a crack, and then she would ask the person what they wanted!

Indian healers? There were some. They're the reason a lot of people survived. I had one cure me. I was really ill. My head got cold and I really got sick. My head was driving me crazy. Next thing I knew, I could barely walk. That's when I went to see one of the medicine men. He didn't do too much. He rubbed me here [pointing to his temples] with some powder. The powder was sort of yellow/brown. That was it! After that I was fine. He just told me to keep still for a while. The only other thing I know of that people did when someone got sick was to give them an enema. This was done quite a bit. I don't know of any other procedures. The Indian healers were successful in their cures.

Richard Beardy. Some of the Indians knew how to be healers, like for some illnesses that weren't too serious. They knew what to use. There was this old lady whose son-in-law accidentally shot himself. This happened up-river on the Hayes. That's where this guy had his accident. Up the river, a ways into the bush. This guy's name was Noah Thomas. Well, this old lady was a healer and she said to bring this Noah down the riverbank to the shore. She said she could help him. Anyway I don't know what she did but she healed him! I often wonder about that. Noah lived to be an old man, you know.

Catherine Anderson. After the white doctors arrived, their medicine was used. The white man's medicine was used and the Indian medicine was forgotten. The Indian doctor used to travel from place to place, visiting elders and healing people. He carried with him an old book. It had a list of herbs and flowers and their uses. This was written in Cree. This person would know what cures to use for whatever illness. These cures and healings were kept to each individual healer. These people stayed at York Factory during the summer. They lived there during the summer.

Sometimes, in the winter, these people would come to York Factory. The ones from Sturgeon River. They came all the way from Sturgeon River to York Factory during the winter! This was just before Christmas.

Abel Chapman. When a person got sick, for instance, if they had a bad stomach-ache, a potion was made from herbs. The red willow was used. The bark is peeled off the willow and put into boiling water. Then the person who is sick would drink this. This didn't take long to work. It cleaned the person out. All the herbs were used for different illnesses. There was no modern medicine. If you cut your finger or accidentally injured yourself with an axe, the person would chew on *kâkikêpakwa* leaves. Then the leaves are put on the wound and bandaged. The wound would heal. The person got well. Same thing with tobacco. You can use it for wounds. All the potions were made from herbs. Like the doctors today know what to give a person for whatever sickness. That's how the people were back then. There were the elders. They knew what to do. The most powerful plant for healing was the one called *kâkikêpakwa.* I once heard an elder talk about this plant, the *kâkikêpakwa,* and what it can cure. If a person had a sore chest, it's applied to the chest. If a young woman had problems with menstruation these leaves were boiled to make a drink and this made the person well. This plant cured them. No modern medicine. The elders knew which plants to use. If a person had a sore throat, pine cones were used. Not old cones, fresh new ones. They were usually red in colour. If a person sucked this in their mouth, their throat gets better. [*Wîhkês*[89]], that's another that is used. For a cold. When a person has a cold. You slice it thinly and put it in hot water. Then you drink the liquid. That's still used today. After you drink the liquid the person feels a lot better in no time. Beer is the only thing that never cures anything!!

Flora Beardy. Were there doctors at York Factory a long time ago. What did people do when someone got sick?
Elizabeth Oman. Nothing. You would die.[90]

Amy Hill. The story that I'm going to tell you was told to me by my late father. He remembered what happened and was one of ten told about it. His mother had given birth to a set of twins.

They were girls. He said this one day his father became a mad-
man. He was going crazy![91] He said the babies were strapped to
cradleboards which were beside the bed. His father was holding
his head and he said that if one of the twins was sacrificed then
he would get better! This was the only way his sanity would
return was if one of the twins was sacrificed. His father told the
rest of the children to lie on the bed, to cover their faces, and not
to look. So they did this and they all heard their father say that
it was time. Nobody moved. There wasn't anyone there to stop
him. The baby was choked; it died. This is one story that my
father told me. I'll always remember this. That's why I think that
what has happened in my family and what is happening now is
because of my grandfather's actions.[92]

A lot of these sicknesses came from the white man and also
from their food. They put all sorts of things into their food. A
long time ago the people rarely got sick from the food they ate. If
a person got sick, it wasn't for very long. They'd get well in no
time. But it's not like that now.

DESCRIPTIONS OF YORK FACTORY

Alex Ouscan. They built a place where the boats were kept for the
winter. They worked in the mud, close to the cemetery. Just
down-river a little ways. All you could see was mud where they
were working. They had a hard time because the mud is frozen
underneath. Yes, it was hard work because the mud was frozen.
They would drag all the soft mud out. They worked all summer.
The Hudson's Bay Company boss thought that they wouldn't finish the job, but they did. The boat would be pulled up there for
the winter. Boats often got wrecked by the ice, if they were left
out close to the river.[93]

Joseph Saunders. Another thing too. The reason why it was so dry,
where the people lived, was because they made ditches farther
back in the bush. I used to see them do this, when I was young.
The ditches used to be about this wide [indicating a measurement
of about four feet in width]. The ditches they had around the
cemetery and the ditches they had around the houses, including

the depot area, went all the way into the bush. They would meet here, back in the bush. That's why it was so dry and that's probably why there wasn't that much erosion on the riverbank.[94]

Richard Beardy. And this building was where they kept the [dog] food.[95] When you had dogs at that time, they were important and had to be well taken care of. Dog food had to be available and looked after. Dog teams were an important way to travel then.

The First Airplanes

Elizabeth Oman. This one time, it was at night. We were already asleep when Sam Saunders came and woke everyone up. He said there was a loud noise out over the water and he said that someone was going to drop something on us! I didn't know what he was talking about. I didn't understand at that time. Anyway, we went outside and I could hear a plane. Flying far from land, over the water. The old people didn't know that it was an airplane. They thought it was something else!

Fred Beardy. At that time there were quite a few people living at Port Nelson and I guess this plane went there first. The plane circled there for some time, probably looking at the area. There was this old man that lived at Port Nelson, Solomon, Solomon Wastesecoot was his name, and when he saw the plane he ran for his rifle! I guess he said, "It's a Thunderbird! That's a Thunderbird and I'm going to shoot it! They say this bird has rich oil!" That's what this old man did when he saw his first plane.

Archelaus Beardy. [When I saw an airplane for the first time] I wondered what in the world it could be. This was on a Sunday and I was on my way to church. I was by the building where they built boats, when I heard the plane. I didn't know what on earth made this sound! I just hugged the side of the building and watched the plane. But that plane at York Factory didn't look anything like the planes today. It looked more like a canoe with wings. It had wings right on the top plus another set on top of these. It had two sets of wings and the body looked like a canoe. The men on the plane had nice clothes on. They had buttons on their jackets just like the buttons my father had on his chieftain jacket. These men stayed and danced at York Factory for two nights before they left.[96]

Joseph Saunders. No, we weren't there at that time when the first plane arrived at York Factory. We heard about it. I guess it was on a Sunday and people were just going to church. It was snowing a bit and visibility was poor. All of a sudden everyone heard this big noise in the sky! They scattered everywhere, running here and there. They were all afraid and thought the world was coming to an end! The plane scared everyone. That's what happened when the first plane arrived at York Factory. When another plane came to York Factory, we were there then. This plane came from Norway House. The plane brought some women into York Factory earlier and came back to pick them up. These women were nurses. We were there when this plane came to York Factory. It stayed out on the river. They had to take an anchor out to keep the plane from drifting away. The plane had two sets of wings, one on top of the other.

The Disrespectful Clerks

Joseph Saunders. At York Factory, I was a young boy then but I remember it well: Mr Faries was the minister at York Factory and he was already living up the river.[97] His mother was still alive then. The day was a Saturday when these four clerks went to visit the minister. I guess these clerks said to Mr Faries's mother: "This is the last time you're going to see us, grandmother. We're going to go hunting tomorrow." They were being disrespectful by hunting on a Sunday. Mrs Faries talked with them and told them not to do that. She said: "Don't go hunting on Sunday. You're not in need of food." Mr Faries also talked to them and told them they shouldn't do that. Anyway, these four clerks went ahead and hunted that Sunday. They went to this creek across the Hayes River and hunted. However, there was an old man living at this creek. He fished there all the time. I guess these clerks went there and gave the old man a hard time. Afterward, the clerks were talking about heading back and this was just before the tide turned to come in. The old man told them not to go yet. He said to wait until the tide goes out. He said it's rough out there when the tide starts going out. The wind is blowing into the mouth of the river. It will be too rough! I guess these fellows didn't want to listen. They took the old man's bannock, broke it into pieces, and threw it at him. Finally, two fellows listened and stayed behind while the other two headed back. Anyway, this canoe came across and went toward the end of the island.[98] They headed straight across the river. And when they got in the middle where the current is the strongest, I saw their canoe tip over. I saw one person, just for a short while, waving his arms, and I saw the other one by the tipped canoe. He dragged himself on top of the canoe. I saw him there just for a while and then he was gone. They both drowned. These clerks destroyed themselves.

Hunger on the Trail

Alex Ouscan. We travelled from York Factory in the fall, along the coast and inland, up the Deer River, which is at Mile 445.[99] We just about starved at that time. We were making our way back to York Factory and we had no food. Everyone was getting pretty hungry. We just kept on walking and walking, eating anything we could chew on or catch. Sometimes we would catch a whiskey jack and eat that. There weren't too many of these around and not too much to them. Not even any ptarmigans. We were getting pretty hungry and desperate. My old grandfather, before our trip, had trapped and skinned a beaver. He had the beaver skin with him and we all ate that. That's how hungry we were! He hadn't dried the pelt; it was just rolled up, frozen. He took this out and we ate it! After, we just kept on walking, heading for York Factory with no food to eat. At one point my late mother tracked a ptarmigan and followed the tracks right to where the ptarmigan awoke from. As she was following the tracks she was picking up the ptarmigan's droppings. We stopped and made a fire and boiled some water. She then put the droppings into the boiling

water and stirred it. This is what she gave me to drink! After that
we just kept on going and pretty soon we were getting close to
York Factory. By this time my late father could hardly walk. He
was so weak from hunger that he fainted. We were about ten
miles away. My uncle Edwin, who was travelling with us, decided to go on ahead by himself. He was trying to reach this one
cabin. He knew the cabin that was there had food in it. My uncle
left us and said he would be back the next day. The next morning
we kept looking for him and finally we saw him coming! We
were so happy to see him coming! He managed to bring some
food back for us. Tea, flour, and lard. He gave these to us and left.
He started ahead of us for York Factory. My mother started cooking and my late grandfather said to not give too much food to my
father.

Chased by a Polar Bear

Alex Ouscan. My grandfather once told me a story about a polar
bear. This happened in the summer and the place where he was
was thick with willows. Anyway, he met a bear and the bear
started chasing him! He didn't have time to load his gun to shoot
the bear. He said he would hide in the willows and the bear
would just throw itself on top of the willows, flattening them. He
was looking for my grandfather! The bear kept after him so he
couldn't load his gun. Anyway this carried on for some time but
he finally managed to get some distance between himself and the
bear, and he was able to load his gun. When he was loading his
gun he dropped his gun flints! By the time he found one, the bear
was on its way towards him! All he found was one cap and all he
had in his gun was one ball. The gun was a double barrel and all
he was able to load was one barrel. Anyway, he was able to get to
a small clearing and when he looked up the bear was standing on
its hind legs, not far from him, with its mouth wide open! The
bear was close to him so he fired into the bear's mouth. That was
it! He killed the bear right there. I can imagine what a polar
bear's like when it is wounded. In this case it wasn't wounded.
My grandfather wasn't bothering the bear. He just ran when it
chased him!

Ship's Candies

Richard Beardy. At York Factory there used to be a long dock there. The schooner would anchor at the end of the dock. Well, sometimes when the ship came in the captain would be in a big hurry to set out again, so the ship had to be unloaded right away. Anyway, this ship came in and the captain gave orders to start unloading right away. There was a lot of cargo to unload because he had been to a few places before reaching York Factory. The captain said that because he wanted to leave as soon as possible, the women would also help unload the ship! It was starting to get dark already so the women agreed to help unload the boat. They carried what they could. The goods were mostly in boxes, but they weren't very big, and the candies were in tubs. The women knew this so they broke one of the tubs on purpose. Boy, there were candies all over the place! That's what I meant by lots of fun when the ship came in!

Mîsîwikitik and his Ten Wives

Richard Beardy. It's true that [my grandfather Robert Beardy] had ten wives. My father travelled with him once. This was when they were hunting black bears, during the season when they are fat. My grandfather always killed two bears. From these two bears he was able to render lots of oil as well as meat. My father said: "The old man would take most of the meat. I guess he needed more because he had ten wives to feed!" I was told that my grandfather didn't love all his wives. There was one he really cared for; she was special to him. She was a short woman. He named her *Cahkokâp.*[100] This was the one he really favoured. He enjoyed travelling with her. Even when he went trapping marten, he would never leave her behind.

Sometimes, at York Factory, they used to fire the cannons. You know the ones that used to be in front of the depot building?[101] Well, I guess my grandfather was on his way back to York Factory from his trapline. Anyway, they saw him coming so they loaded the cannons to get them ready for firing. Just before he got to shore they would fire the cannons. This old man was important because he had so many wives. I guess at that time the more women you had and took care of, the more honourable a man was! The firing of the cannons would make my grandfather very happy.

But I was told that it was his wives that did all the work for him! He would take three wives to *Wâpistânihk* [Place of Martens], and then the wives would find poles to set up the rest of the dwelling. He, *Mîsîwikitik*,[102] would help sometimes. When this was done he would get two wives to set marten traps. The other wife, the one he loved, would go along with him, leaving the other two behind. When he got to his destination, then he and his wife would build a place for themselves. He would never leave her behind!

They raised pigs at York Factory. Boy, they were noisy! They would unload them off the ship and the pigs would squeal. The guys used to hit them! They're tough! When it was calm out, no wind, you can hear these pigs squealing from a long ways. Anyway, there was this one old lady from God's Lake who was really afraid of these pigs. I guess someone told her that if a live pig licks a person, that person will get sick. They were just teasing her but she believed them! She was afraid of these pigs and when she saw someone near them she would say: "Watch out! You better watch out! The pigs might lick you!"

Learning by Experience

Mary Redhead. The kids were out on this flat rock and they had just finished dancing. Anyway the tide was coming in and they were out on this flat rock. They were standing on this rock, not realizing that the tide was coming in! So I told my husband, "Those kids are going to get stranded out there." I wanted him to call out to them but he said: "Just wait. Don't say anything yet. They'll realize right away what's happening." So I didn't say anything. The boys were busy watching a seal swimming in the river. My husband said: "They'll find out in a minute to listen to what they were told! They were told to always watch out for the incoming tide." Frank was standing there too with the boys. The seal they were watching dove under and when it popped up again, it was right in front of them. You should have seen them.

They started yelling, turned around to run for shore. Well, that's when they saw all the water around them so they had to wade through the water! They didn't take long to get to shore. They got scared of the seal. At that time, the chief was my late uncle Abraham Beardy. He was standing on shore laughing at the boys. He told them they wouldn't have been in that situation if they had listened to what they were told. Everyone that was watching laughed at them!

Mr Faries's Bull and Cow

Elizabeth Oman. The late Mr Faries had a bull and a cow. That bull used to chase people! We used to be scared to go and visit, over where the Shamattawa people used to camp, on account of that bull.

Amy Hill. This bull [of Mr Faries] was wicked! The school house we went to was a small building. One day, when we were inside, something started kicking the door. Yes! It was the bull kicking the door! The teacher pulled the door open and grabbed the bull around the neck. The bull ran off with the teacher hanging on to its neck! We were watching from the school. Some of the children were so afraid that they ran away. The bull would shake its head but the teacher hung on! With everyone yelling, it wasn't too long before we saw Mr Faries running towards the bull, shaking his stick in the air. We thought maybe the teacher was hurt, but he wasn't. Yes, that bull was wicked!

The Omen of the Rabbit

Albert Hill. I went to check my rabbit snares and I got one rabbit. This was at Shamattawa. I walked back across the river on the ice towards home. I decided to take a rest, so I sat down and laid the rabbit right beside me. The rabbit's coat was all frosted and its head was all covered with snow. It was dead. As I went to pick up the rabbit, it was gone! I noticed the tracks leading away and when I looked up I saw it running away! There was this one old woman that told us something's going to happen in your family. The rabbit was a sign. Not too long after, your [Flora Beardy's] father arrived and brought us the bad news. This is what this old woman had told us. She said that when someone arrived here, that person will have bad news. So it wasn't too long after that your father arrived. He told me: "It's your father. You do not have a father any more." That is what he said. That's why I had this sign.

It is a good power to have, to be able to know what these signs mean. But sometimes the omens can be bad.

Amy Hill. Yes, because it involves spirits.

Albert Hill. Not that anything would happen to the person who receives these signs; the spirits are usually friendly but knowing that someone in the family is going to die is the hard part. Some people are not able to handle this. This is what is called the ghost/spirit omen. This is what it was called, a long time ago.

Spared by a Polar Bear

Abel Chapman. There's a story about this person who was disrespectful to the polar bear. This person teased the animal. The bear chased him and caught up with him. The bear flattened this fellow to the ground and tore part of his scalp. This bear then got off the fellow and walked away. He had torn the scalp off this person! This fellow was crying "That's enough! You're killing me!" to the polar bear. The people say the polar bear understands when you talk to it. That's when the bear let him go. The bear let him go. The fellow just lay there until the bear was a good distance away! That's when he got up. He wrapped his head and walked back to his home. He was alright after. He didn't die.

Power and Bad Feelings

Abel Chapman. John George was the oldest brother to Archelaus and Richard Beardy. He was married for a short time before he died. They say that someone who disliked or was jealous of him was responsible for his death. That was the one bad thing that people did to each other a long time ago. Of all of us that are here, I guess we can say we survived! There were some that hated others and had the power to harm them. But I don't think there are too many of them left today. At least ones that are my age. Maybe a few. This was a terrible thing. You were careful about how you treated others. People made sure they didn't make others angry. This was how it was, how some people were. These people will be faced with this on their judgment day. Even if you are not a mean person to others and you have to work hard to get by, if someone makes you very angry your feelings will change. You will also show/feel great anger towards this person. Even if you don't have these powers, if you keep thinking/wishing the other person harm, it will eventually happen! That's how this works.

First Contact with the Hudson's Bay Company

Abel Chapman. This is a story that was told to [my grandfather] by an elder. This person was talking about Kaskatamagun. This was a long time ago. There were Indians living there but there was no store, no such thing as salt or oats. Everyone trapped for fur. Their food came from the land, fish from the rivers. This was a long, long time ago. This is what he [my grandfather] used to tell me. The elder went on to say that there were quite a few families living there. One day they saw something way out in the bay. This was the first contact with the Natives by the company![103] I guess there was a boat coming closer to shore. A lot of the people ran and hid! They were afraid, so they ran and hid. The men pulled to shore but they had someone to interpret for them. The interpreter said that the company was looking for Natives to trade with. These men took all the fur the Indians had accumulated and unloaded a lot of trade items. Things that were never seen or used at that time but are used today. That's when trading in that area began and in York Factory. This was many years ago. A long time ago.

Keeping our Way of Life

Richard Beardy. Lots of times I sit and think about a long time ago. What I remember and saw. How people survived and what they did to survive. Today things are so different. It's a lot easier for people today. This is what we were told a long time ago and we remember this. We were told that in the future things were going to be different; there would be changes. I see a bit of this today. We were also told that some day the Indian culture and way of life will be forgotten. There will be changes; things will happen differently. We were told, in the past, not to lose our way of life, our heritage, to practise it always. Not to lose touch with our culture. We were also told, when we first started going to meetings down south, that the white men were trying to change the Indians, trying to get them to live the way they do. But it's not going to be like that, at least not soon. Maybe way in the future. Today, there's still a lot of Indians hanging onto their way of life, their culture. It's different in the north than in the south. In the south it's easier to live the way the white men do.

ANCIENT LEGENDS AND TRADITIONS

Wîsahkêcâhk and the Dancing Birds

Abel Chapman. As Wîsahkêcâhk[104] walked on, he saw a lake ahead of him. He kept hidden for he wanted to check the lake. There he saw a lot of animals! He spied on them. There were lots of geese and ducks. All sorts of birds. He decided he wanted to eat some, but he had no gun so he couldn't shoot them. He had to figure out some way of catching these birds. With Wîsahkêcâhk, there was no shortage of ways to trick others. So he went into the bush and made himself a bag and filled it with moss. This he carried on his back. Then he started walking along the shore of the lake where all the birds were. He took his time. "Wîsahkêcâhk, what is that you are carrying?" the birds asked. "It is my songs," Wîsahkêcâhk answered. "My songs that I am carrying." "Well, play the songs!" the birds said. "No. No, I can't play the songs just anywhere!" Wîsahkêcâhk replied. "I can only play them inside a wigwam!" He slowly kept on walking. Then the birds said, "We'll build a wigwam so we can hear your songs!" They all started to build and built a large wigwam. When it was completed all the ducks and geese went inside and also all the other birds. The loon too. Wîsahkêcâhk said: "You must do what the song says. You must do exactly what the song says!" The birds all started singing! Then they started dancing! Just like today people sing and dance. You see it on TV. The song said, "Close your eyes and keep your heads down." All the birds closed their eyes and danced in a big circle! They had their heads down. As they passed by *Wîsahkêcâhk* he would grab one of the birds and wring its neck! Soon he had quite a few birds. He didn't want the birds to open their eyes.

But it was the loon that opened one eye. He saw what *Wîsahkêcâhk* was doing and cried out, "*Wîsahkêcâhk* is killing us!" All the birds opened their eyes and ran out of the wigwam. When the loon was running out *Wîsahkêcâhk* stepped on its back and broke it! That's why the loon looks the way it does. He killed lots of birds before the loon caught on! So he gathered up all the birds he killed. The rest had run away. He carried all his birds away and went to build a big fire. He stuck all the birds into the sand, just the feet were sticking out. This is how he cooked the birds.

While he waited for the birds to cook he decided to nap. He lay with his rear facing the fire. He instructed his rear end to wake him up if someone was trying to steal his birds. But his rear end did not do this. It did not wake up *Wîsahkêcâhk* when thieves arrived and ate all his birds. They ate all the birds and stuck the feet back into the sand, to make it look like the birds were still in the ground. *Wîsahkêcâhk* woke up very hungry and decided to eat. He pulled out a pair of feet and there was no bird on it! He pulled the rest out and found that all his birds had been eaten. *Wîsahkêcâhk* was very angry. Very angry! He started scolding his rear end! His rear end made him mad because the rear end didn't tell him of the thieves! *Wîsahkêcâhk* said, "Just you wait rear end, just wait, I'll get even with you!" *Wîsahkêcâhk* proceeded to build a big fire around a big rock. Soon the rock was red hot. *Wîsahkêcâhk* started rubbing his rear end on the rock! He was burning his rear end on the rock! This was his way of getting even with his rear end! He said, "Aha! Good for you, rear end"! That's how angry he was! So *Wîsahkêcâhk* went on his way, his rear end smarting. He couldn't kill anything because his rear end was making too much noise! Poo! Poo! Poo! Soon he was starting to worry. By now huge scabs had formed on his rear end. He was very hungry and now he was thinking of eating the scabs. So he continued to do so. While he was eating someone spoke to him, "*Wîsahkêcâhk*, what is that you are eating?" *Wîsahkêcâhk* an-swered, "It's my mother's dried meat! She made it mixed with blood!"

Wîsahkêcâhk, Kayânwî, Wêmisôs, and *Cahkâpês.*[105] There are lots of legends about them that my grandmother used to tell me. That's how the children were back then. They'd all sit together and listen to these stories. My grandmother used to tell these leg-ends. My grandmother, my mother's mother, did not tell stories. The grandmother that told us legends was my father's mother.

The Rabbit Husband and the Frog Wife

Abel Chapman. This legend is about a rabbit that was married to a frog. The frog said to her husband the rabbit, "It's time for you to go hunting." So the rabbit made himself a pair of snowshoes to hunt with. The rabbit has big feet so I don't know why he needed snowshoes! Anyway the rabbit left. He went hunting. In a very short time he returned. He said he saw a big, frightful animal. He was afraid of it so he didn't kill it! So the frog said, "Let me try." The frog went hopping away. That's all the frog does is hop! The big animal was still there. It was a moose! So the frog hopped in-side the moose's rear end and travelled through the passageways until it reached a vital organ. The frog bit the vital organ and killed the moose![106] The frog was the one to kill the moose! Yes, the rabbit's wife killed the moose. Then the rabbit said to his wife: "What would you do if a pack of wolves were to come? How would you save yourself?" His wife the frog replied: "Where the blood has melted the snow is where I will bury myself, deep into the ground". The rabbit replied: "Oh, I shall hop around and run away. When I get tired I shall crawl into the moose carcass!" The rabbit hopped around and before long was tired, so he crawled into the moose carcass. Soon the wolves arrived and ate the whole moose carcass and the poor rabbit. He thought he'd be safe inside the moose carcass. The frog kept herself alive by digging into the ground.

The Origin of the Months

Abel Chapman. A long time ago, not long after life began, the ani-mals all got together and had a meeting. *Wîsahkêcâhk* asked each animal how many moons there should be. *Atik*, the caribou, said there should be as many moons as the hair on my coat! For sure there would have been many moons! Then he was told: "No, that is too many. You would not live very long." Soon all the animals had their say and the last one to speak was the frog. Well, the frog has six toes on each foot. So the frog was told to speak. The frog said, "There should be as many moons as I have toes." After great thought *Wîsahkêcâhk* said, "So be it." The frog's suggestion was taken. The frog has six toes on each foot which is why there are twelve months to a year! Goodness, the caribou wanted as many moons as hair on its coat!

SEASONAL LIFE IN THE YORK FACTORY AREA

Alex Ouscan. [The people] travelled in groups and they looked after each other. That's what they used to do. They would travel around during the winter, moving from camp to camp and trapping at the same time, understand? They would also hunt for their food as they travelled. Like, for instance, caribou. If they killed lots of caribou, they would stay at that camp for a longer period.

Abel Chapman. Everybody left [their traplines] and stayed for the summer at York Factory. Nobody stayed at their traplines during the summer, July and August. People started leaving in September for all different places, to their traplines; then some would return at Christmas and some families a little earlier. It wasn't hardship for the elders to travel in those days. Not like today. Everyone seems to have a hard time getting around. That's true! Back then you see the elders travelling, walking. Some were probably in their nineties.

If the woman is alone, her husband has died, she's the one that looks after herself. She does everything for herself. Yes, she hunts to feed herself. She's able to do everything! Today some of the elders don't do this. They're just like the young people who aren't interested in hunting for themselves.

Elizabeth Oman. We never travelled from there [York Factory] until after our mother died. We'd go with our father to other places.

He worked for the Hudson's Bay Company. He was a trader. He would go pick up fur from the trappers.[107] And also go and give the people food supplies like flour, tea, sugar, lard – things like that. Butter. We went and wintered at this place. Let's see ... It was called Sturgeon Lake. You have to go up-river towards Shamattawa and you pass Shamattawa to get there. My father also worked at Shamattawa. He looked after the store there.

People came [to York Factory] from Shamattawa to spend the summer. From Shamattawa, the Indians. The people would go and stay at Kaskatamagun for the winter. Then they'd move here [York Factory] toward the summer, and then they'd go back in the fall. They travelled by boat, using paddles. [In the fall] every-body moved away, the whole family. All the families from York Factory. To that place, Kaskatamagun. Old people too.

Archelaus Beardy. My father had a big house [at Wanatawahak], a big house. It had two storeys. He built it himself. All he used was an axe. He would chop down the trees, take the bark off, and use the axe to make the logs square. He would start chopping early in the morning, as long as he can see his axe, and work until he couldn't see anything at night! It didn't take him long to finish his house. Nobody helped him, he did it by himself.

We would go up the Hayes River as far as the Pennycutaway River.[108] Then we would travel up this river. It's quite far. We would stay there and trap during the winter. Then in the late spring, after breakup, we would build a raft and come down the Pennycutaway using the raft and sail. We would stop where the Pennycutaway meets the Hayes River. Usually when we get to the Hayes River, it hasn't broken up yet and there would be a lot of water on top of the ice. In some places the ice would be piled quite high! Then we would come down the Hayes River [to York Factory].

David Massan. When I lived there, there were lots of people at Big Trout Lake. At that time, there were no such things as houses. There were no supplies brought there to build houses. Like ply-wood. But there were nails, stoves, roofing tarp, and window-panes. This is what the Hudson's Bay Company brought in if they were going to build a house. The Indians lived in wigwams

Alex and Martha Chapman and family at York Factory, *c.* 1932. Abel Chapman
(wearing hat) is at the far left. (Courtesy of John Ingram).

and earth homes. During Christmas there would be lots of people at Big Trout Lake and there would be no houses for them. They would just collect tree boughs to sleep on. These people had children with them. Some moved in with family or friends, in the wigwams, if there was room. They would also put up tents to live in and it was cold at that time of year. There would be lots of people arriving there before Christmas. Sometimes steady for two days, there would be people arriving. They came there to go to church. Some travelled great distances, from settlement to settlement. They would use sleds to pull their belongings. Some had dogs to pull their sleds. Most of these families had children with them. They didn't have fur to cover themselves with. I guess all they had was rabbit skins to use for clothing. At that time, they didn't have clothing like we see today. It was a hardship for the Hudson's Bay Company to bring goods to Big Trout Lake. The supplies had to come from Fort Severn and it was a long hard trip.

Archelaus Beardy. There were quite a few of us [at Wanatawahak] especially in the summer. During summer, this is where the people from Norway House came. They would stay here all summer. They wouldn't go back to Norway House until fall. That's when they would go back. Well we had a store here, it was real big. This was Mr Ray's store.[109] It was almost as big as the Hudson's Bay Company store [at York Factory].

Mary Redhead. Yes, we'd go up-river from Shamattawa. We also stayed at Wanatawahak and went up-river from there for the winter. There were others, from Wanatawahak, who would winter down-river from there. Indians. Everyone left, the whole family and the elders too. I used to set rabbit snares! I would set snares and when I went out with my husband, he showed me how to set traps. That's how we bought a new canoe one spring. I trapped three marten and my husband trapped four!

John Neepin. I was born at Wanatawahak but I don't remember how old I was when we left there. We came to *Pâwinakâw*/Port Nelson and that's where I grew up. We lived there until the time came for me to leave my parents. To live my own life. That's when I left there. I came to Gillam. That's where I got married, at Gillam. I left from York Factory when I realized none of the York Factory women wanted me. I found one in Gillam. We've been together now for almost fifty years!

The people would all leave in the fall and wouldn't be back until Christmas. Sometimes just the men would come back, not the women. But at Easter the whole family would come back.

Amelia Saunders. They had a minister there [Mr Faries at York Factory] all the time. He lived there at York Factory. But where we lived, he would visit every three years. They used to bring the minister by boat in the summer, on the *Mooswa.* And if he came to visit in the winter he would come by dog team. This wasn't too often. The children would all watch when the boat came in and they would also watch when there was a wedding. My grandfather was a minister and when he came to Kaskatamagun from Fort Severn, he would baptize the children. This was before we set out for the winter to go trapping.

Joseph Saunders. A long time ago everyone used to live together. It's only lately, I can't remember what year, that those people moved to Shamattawa.[110] They used to live in the York Factory and Kaskatamagun area. But they stayed in Shamattawa for the winter and came to York Factory in the summer. And as for us, we lived and survived at Kaskatamagun. That area is quite different than living in the bush [inland]. There are no lakes from which to get fish. We got fish from the Kaskatamagun river and also from other small rivers in the area. These were the only places. Everyone spent their time hunting, trapping, and fishing in order to keep alive. Moving from place to place during the winter. We lived mainly on caribou and on beaver which we caught during the winter. There were no moose around there at that time. It's just lately that there's moose there. Yes, everyone spent their time hunting and trapping for food. Life was different living along the coast than living inland. The people who lived inland must have lived along the lakes. They probably survived by fishing. Sometimes life was hard for us, especially if there were no caribou around in the winter. Then we had to hunt for other animals so we could have food. But by spring there was usually a lot to eat. This is when all the birds and other animals start arriving.

TREATIES AND TREATY DAYS

John Neepin. During "the time of money"[111] at York Factory, everyone who left York Factory for the winter came back at this time. People from Shamattawa and the Kaskatamagun area. There weren't that many people from Kaskatamagun. Then there was us, from Port Nelson. In the later years there weren't too many of us left. Earlier there were lots of us at Port Nelson. There were lots of people at Port Nelson at one time. Then after the time of great sickness,[112] there were a lot less people. There weren't very many of us left. This was one thing the Indians used to do. They would all gather together during the time of money. They had a feast during the time of money. The people saved the food that they'd need at this time and sometimes bring in other food like ... meat, dried meat, pemmican, flour, and maybe salt pork, tea, sugar. At that time just money was given. There would also be a trader there. To sell goods during the time of money. The store, then, did not look anything like the store today. Lots of things they didn't have. There was no meat, no eggs.

Mary Redhead. As far as I can remember the chiefs always dressed nice on Treaty Day. They wore nice jackets. The councillors also dressed the same as the chiefs. They had jackets with yellow stripes on their sleeves. Whatever the occasion they would always wear these. Council meetings, court hearings. The chiefs today don't do that.

That's when we would take different items to York Factory to trade/sell. The trader knew what items to take. He had things like oranges. Things that were sweet and also potatoes. I remember these. These were the things people bought mostly. Things were not expensive then. You were able to purchase quite a bit for five dollars.

Oh, they would have a dance [on Treaty Day]. Yes, I used to see them have dances. Oh they would have a big dance! There were lots of good dancers, good music! At that time they had different

Chief Charles Wastasecoot and councillors after signing Treaty Five at York Factory, 10 August 1910. (Provincial Archives of Manitoba, A.V. Thomas Collection, 133).

square dances. Everyone danced to them! They always had this dance, *napatêsimowin*. It was a square dance. The women would line up on one side and the men on the opposite side. They would go around in a circle and swing each other. It was nice to watch! They always had a feast every year on Treaty Day. Everyone would eat. When everyone was finished eating, then the dancing would start, usually towards evening. They didn't stop until morning! They danced until they were tired and sleepy! Some would even sleep at the dance hall! Yes, that's what they did. They played football all the time. It was mainly dancing and the feast on Treaty Day. The men who challenged each other would get tea and bannock after the game. They used to say that one of the [HBC] bosses started this. He would give everyone tea and bannock and the winners were allowed to have a dance for everyone!

Catherine Anderson. The Mounties gave the money out.[113] Oh, you should have seen them! They were dressed in red and they had guns on them. The long guns. The strap came around the front and the gun sat on their back. The RCMP asked me to dance so I did! They were all sitting in a row, watching me, while I danced! First I had to put my socks and shoes on because I was barefoot.

Archelaus Beardy. They would have dances and games [at treaty time]. I don't know if they had a real feast. Just mainly dancing. The court-house or band hall was a big building and that's where they used to have the dance. They would dance until morning and until they were tired!

The Mounties would travel with the Indian agent and the treaty party from place to place and one would be dressed in red. They also had a doctor in the treaty party. I think the doctor was deaf. He had a hard time hearing. I don't know why he was a doctor; he couldn't hear!

Joseph Saunders. It was during this time of money that we were given small amounts of food. Not lots, just a little bit. Salt pork, one slab was about this size.[114] This is what people ate mainly. *Amelia Saunders.* It had thick skin and we would boil it. It tasted real good.

Royal North-West Mounted Police patrol and others during the payment of treaty annuities at York Factory, July 1914. (Provincial Archives of Manitoba, J.G. Jones Collection, 59).

The Reverend Richard and Catherine Faries (right) with local people after the signing of Treaty Five at York Factory in August 1910. (Provincial Archives of Manitoba).

Joseph Saunders. Yes, it tasted real good. They used to keep it in a barrel.

Amelia Saunders. They also had ice and salt in the barrels. It tasted real good.

Joseph Saunders. [We also received] flour, raisins, and white beans.

Amelia Saunders. Sugar.

Joseph Saunders. And other things, things like files. Sometimes we got a knife.

Amelia Saunders. Thick rope and wool blankets. The ones they call *okimow* blankets.[115]

Joseph Saunders. Fishing hooks too [and] five dollars.

David Massan. The children were also involved. They had hopping games. The old people too. They would take a sack and hop around in it! A sack race. Sometimes they fell down! They also had foot races. They didn't have too much going on during Treaty Day, just these games. I never saw them do things like carrying things on their backs, flour packing. I never saw that.

Abel Chapman. My late father used to bring the treaty party here [to York Factory] to give treaty when they first started giving out money. My grandfather told me this. I think they went to three different places. This [Churchill] was one. He [my grandfather] used to mention the promises made to the Indians when the treaty was signed. There would be the chief and usually two councillors. The Indian agent and RCMP. The promise to provide for the Natives is in the treaty and signed. Promises to last as long as the grass grew, the rivers ran and the sun shone. This is the promise that was made. To an Indian this means forever.

GRANDFATHERS AND GRANDMOTHERS

John Neepin. The elders would talk about their travels when they were young, what they remember. The Indians didn't worry too much about anything. They were happy as long as they had food for their families. And the elders, they rarely got sick a long time

ago. Not like now. I used to hear my late father say that today so
many elders are always sick. As far as I can remember, the elders
I've known, I never knew of the old people getting sick. When an
elder got sick a long time ago, then you knew that this person
was old and was probably going to die. That's what he used to
tell me. That's how it was.

I barely remember my grandfathers. I know I saw them but
I barely remember them. There's one that I don't remember the
name of. I remember my mother was holding me and this person
wanted to pick me up! But I hid behind my mother's back! It was
an old man and I was afraid of him. He'd reach out towards me.
I guess he wanted to kiss me but I was afraid of him. My mother
kept saying, "That's your grandfather!" I didn't think of him as
a grandfather. I was afraid of him and considered him a *mahîhkan*![116]

Mary Redhead. Oh yes! [The elders] helped with the children. The
babies would be in their *tihkinâkans*.[117] Even when they were able
to walk they'd be tied in the cradle.

David Massan. The old people were a lot stronger and tougher a
long time ago. Even when they were at an old age they were still
able to walk. They were healthy. Not too many people got sick.
There weren't too many known sicknesses or people getting sick.
When an old person was ready to die, it was just like they wanted
to sleep. No suffering involved. Mostly they just lie down and go
to sleep and never wake up.

Joseph Saunders. Oh, they [the elders] stayed home. They often
looked after the children while the women were outside working
or out hunting. The grandparents a long time ago talked to the
children and prayed together with them, as far as I can remember. Times were a lot more serene then, not like today. In the
evening before sundown, everyone would take their children
inside. With the whole family together prayers were said and
then everyone went to bed. Also prayers were said first thing in
the morning. Also, when people were together visiting you can
hear them singing hymns in the homes and praying together.
Again, prayers were said in the morning. Everyone rested well at

night. It was always quiet and peaceful. If there was someone in the community who was real sick, there would be someone with that person, praying and caring for them. People never fought with each other. They didn't call or put each other down. They got along well and respected each other.

Abel Chapman. I was a lot younger then so I just lived and worked from day to day. But now that I'm older it's a lot different. You have a lot of time to think about life, about death, the past, how much longer I have left on this earth. It's a very solitary feeling. I often think about the past and where we used to live, the life, and I really miss it. This is how it is with me. I remember a long time ago seeing an elder sitting, without talking. The person must have been thinking, reminiscing. This is what they were doing! I know now because I do that a lot! I used to wonder why they would sit there and not say anything but now I know why.

The elders today don't pay as much attention to the young people, as in the past. The other thing is the youngsters don't like to be given advice. A long time ago the youngsters gathered around an elder, like we sit around the TV today. The elder would relate stories about survival. That's how the children learned. Listening to elders. If there was one old man who knew how to play the fiddle, he was the teacher and this was passed on from generation to generation. The elders were the teachers in everything.

John Neepin. The one thing I'm happy about today is what I see at meetings. They always ask an elder to say prayers before they start. That's why I'm so pleased. The youngsters often come and ask me to say prayers at their meetings.

LEAVING YORK FACTORY

David Massan. [In 1957] the Indian agent, I can't remember his name, came to York Factory and told us that because there were no jobs at York Factory, maybe we too should leave.[118] That's when we left. We left there to go and look for jobs. We didn't know to what we were going to. We didn't know what the place was like because we'd never been there before.[119] We just left!

Fred Beardy. The summer of 1957 is when I left York Factory. I arrived at the railroad tracks at Weir River, and then we got on the train from there and came to Gillam. From Gillam we went to Ilford and from Ilford to York Landing. We arrived here in the fall [of 1957]. We started building our house as soon as we got here. This was the first house we lived in. Charlie Spence was in charge of this job. He was the one that supervised the first houses that were built here. Old Charlie Spence. And then later I became a carpenter. I worked on the other houses that were being built and I'm still working! [I was] very sorry [to leave]! That's why I always go back there. I miss the place. I always go back there. I went there in 1972, to the goose camp, and I still go there every year. That's about fifteen summers now. It's nice living there. There's no shortage of food.

Abel Chapman. There was this fellow from Split Lake that came to visit me here in Churchill. One time we were having a few drinks at my house and he talked about this [leaving York Factory] also. His name is Lazarus. He said that [York Landing] had to be the worst piece of land that these people were moved to! He went on to say that he often wondered how this happened. Why the person who was in charge let this happen to the people? There's nothing there for them. No hunting. They're surrounded by other smaller settlements on all sides. There's no place for them to go and hunt. It's a very small area and very little hunting. They are unable to survive off the land. They are closed in, in that area. There's Split Lake, Gillam, Ilford, and Thompson. That's four towns surrounding them. They would have been better off settling in a different area. Before you get to where the community is now, there are high riverbanks, a very nice area. I think it would have been nicer there. They would have been able to claim land to the east, closer to the tracks, east of the tracks. There are no towns there. But where they are now, they're completely surrounded. But nobody thought of doing this. That would have been a better place for them to relocate to. Also it was the doctor's fault. His name was Joe. He was the doctor at York Factory at that time and was also the "Big Boss" as he was called. McIvor.[120] It was these people who forced the move. They said it was too expensive for the plane to keep flying into the area. They spend more money today to keep people on social assistance at York Landing. Even for one person for one year! At York Factory, people weren't on social assistance. People who lived there were able to feed themselves.

Catherine Anderson. This one thing I heard a long time ago, when I was young. One chief was talking about the future and what would happen if his people didn't listen. His one wish was that the people wouldn't leave the York Factory area. When the people moved from York Factory there were lots of problems. The elder chief's wish was not respected. He did not want the people to leave that area. Now today there's nobody there. People were happy at York Factory. All the old folks are passing on. I don't think there's too many alive today.

They just took a few things with them [when York Factory closed]. The people were told to leave everything! The new chief told them that they would be looked after and given new things, when they arrived at their destination [York Landing]. He told his people this and all this time he was lying to them!

Biographies

The following section contains brief biographies of the fourteen York Factory elders who were interviewed for the York Factory Oral History Project. The biographies list each individual's place of birth, parents, grandparents, spouses, and children, and provide information on their lives at York Factory and their work history. Since these interviews were completed, a number of the elders have passed away. The rest reside in northern Manitoba at Churchill, York Landing, Thompson, Gillam, and Bird.

DAVID MASSAN

David Massan was born at Big Trout Lake, Ontario, on 3 August 1915, the son of Henry Massan and Flora Thomas. He believes that his father, who died at Big Trout Lake in 1928, was born in Ontario but does not know when. David's mother was born at Big Trout Lake and she, too, died there in 1928. His paternal grandparents were Maryjean and James Massan, both from Big Trout Lake. His maternal grandmother's name was Sarah Thomas but David does not know his grandfather's name.

At the age of thirteen David lost both parents and he left his birthplace for York Factory in 1930. The ship did not stop at York, however, and instead went straight to Churchill, to which the railway had by then been completed. From Amery, just north of Gillam, he went by canoe down the Nelson River and finally reached York Factory.

David did not go to school but spent all his life trapping. He lived at York Factory with his aunt Nora Jean Massan. Shortly after arriving he lost his uncle in a drowning accident. On 18 July 1940, David married Jessie Etta Ouscan at York Factory. They did not have any children of their own. The daughter Jessie had prior to her marriage to David is named Salome and is married to George Beardy. She and her family reside in Churchill. David is retired and now lives in Gillam.

CATHERINE ANDERSON

Catherine Anderson was born Catherine Napayokeesik, up-river from Shamattawa, on 2 June 1908, the daughter of John Napayokeesik and Maria Beardy. She does not know when or where her father was born or where he died. Her mother was born at Fort Severn, Ontario. Catherine was very young when her mother died and some years later she lost her father. Her maternal grandparents were Magnus and Mary Beardy, and her paternal grandmother was Mary Napayokeesik.

Raised by Eliza Beardy from Island Lake, Manitoba, who was the widow of Simon Beardy, Catherine lived at Shamattawa, Port Nelson, and York Factory, and briefly attended school during the summers at York Factory. She married Samuel George Anderson at York Factory in August 1925. He was born Samuel George Kakikayapun at Big Trout Lake but took the last name Anderson after his uncle, William Anderson, who raised him. Catherine and Samuel had eight children. Daughters Dorothy Redhead and Jessie Beardy live in Shamattawa; Esther Emily Spence lives in Churchill and is married to Francis Spence. All of Catherine's siblings are deceased.

While Catherine was at York Factory she learned to read the Cree syllabic bible under the supervision of the Reverend Richard Faries. In her later years she resided in the Split Lake nursing home and she passed away there in October 1990.

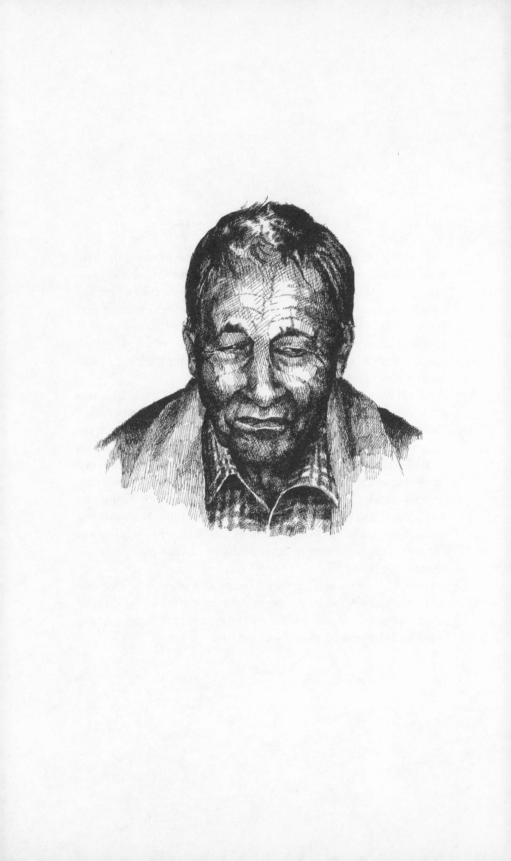

ALEX OUSCAN

Alex Ouscan was born north of York Factory at Wapinayo/White Partridge Creek on the Hudson Bay coast. His father was Abel Ouscan who was born at York Factory and who died at Port Nelson in 1927. His mother was Elizabeth Anderson who was born at Fort Severn on 18 June 1883; she died at the senior citizens' home in Norway House, Manitoba, and was buried at York Landing. His paternal grandfather was Sandy Ouscan but Alex does not know his grandmother's name. Alex's maternal grandparents were Jean and Johnny Anderson. All his grandparents were originally from Fort Severn and they lived at York Factory.

Alex spent the early part of his life hunting and trapping with his family. His first marriage was to Alice Wastesicoot and he has two surviving children from this union. His second marriage, to Caroline Gray, the widow of James Oman, took place in Churchill on 2 December 1972. There were no children born of this marriage.

Alex received very little formal education. Besides trapping and hunting, he learned how to sew clothing and do beadwork. He now makes his home in Thompson. From a family of ten brothers and sisters, he has only one sibling still alive, his brother Roderick who lives in York Landing.

JOSEPH AND AMELIA SAUNDERS

Joseph Saunders was born on 30 January 1907 at Kaskatamagun to Sam Saunders and Mary Thomas. Joseph believes that both his parents were born at Fort Severn, Ontario, and died at York Landing. His paternal grandfather was Jimmy Saunders, but he does not know his grandmother. His maternal grandparents were Maggie and Thomas Thomas and they too were from Fort Severn.

Joseph's early childhood was spent with the family, hunting, trapping, and journeying between Kaskatamagun and York Factory. His formal education was limited to the summertime. He married Amelia Stoney from Fort Severn at York Factory on 31 July 1933, and they had six children. When the time came for their children to go to school, Amelia and Joseph moved to York Factory, leaving Kaskatamagun. After the post at York Factory closed they moved to York Landing. Amelia Saunders passed away there on 20 February 1994.

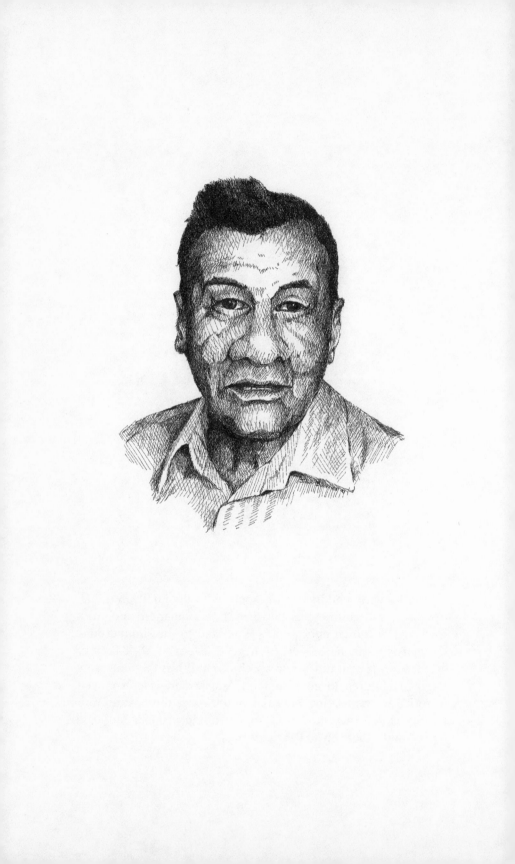

ABEL CHAPMAN

Abel Chapman, an elder of Churchill, was born at Wanatawahak, near York Factory, on 16 June 1922 to Alex and Martha
Chapman. His father was born at Sturgeon River, Ontario, and
died at York Landing at the age of 94. His mother was Martha
Beardy, daughter of Chief Abraham Beardy. She was born not
very far from Shamattawa at a place called *Mêmênitôkanis* and
died at York Landing at age 75. Abel's paternal grandparents
were Phillip and Maggie Chapman and his maternal grandparents were Abraham and Sally Beardy.

Abel was raised by his maternal grandparents until he was
sixteen, at which time he returned to his parents. He did not go to
school, but learned from his grandfather how to hunt, trap, and
survive off the land. Abel came from a large family. Today there
are two surviving: Abel and his brother Douglas who lives at
York Landing. Abel married Amy Neepin at York Factory on
24 August 1942 and they had eight children. They lived at Wanatawahak until they moved to Bird, in 1956. In October that year
Abel joined Canadian National Railways where he worked for
31 years. He is now retired and lives in Churchill.

One of Abel's grandmothers was a storyteller, and he relates,
"the way we sit around a TV today, that is how we children gathered around our grandmother and listened to her stories." He remembers a lot of the legends and does not hesitate to share them
with others.

ARCHELAUS BEARDY

Archelaus Beardy was born at York Factory on 10 February 1912. He was the son of Chief Abraham Beardy, who had been born at Shamattawa in 1878 and who died in 1950 at Whitefish Lake, Manitoba, at the age of 72 years. He was buried at Shamattawa. His mother was Sally Beardy who was born in 1872, also at Shamattawa. She died in 1964 in The Pas, Manitoba, at the age of 92 and was buried at York Landing. Archelaus's paternal grandparents were Magnus and Mary Beardy and his maternal grandparents were Sandy and Mary Beardy, all of whom were from Shamattawa.

Archelaus did not go to school. He learned how to hunt and trap from his father and, like his brother Richard, spent his childhood at Wanatawahak, York Factory, and on the trapline. His first marriage was to Jemima Taylor of Fort Severn. From this union there is one surviving son. His second marriage was to Greta Spence, the daughter of the late Reverend Eli Spence. Of the nine children born to this marriage, six sons and three daughters, there are eight surviving. Archelaus's third marriage was to Florence Outchikat (née Gray), a widow. They had no children.

Archelaus left York Factory in 1953 and was employed with Canadian National Railways. After retiring, he lived in Split Lake, Thompson, and Churchill. Archelaus passed away at Thompson in September 1989 and was laid to rest in Churchill.

FRED BEARDY

Fred Beardy was born at York Factory on 18 April 1919. His father was Josiah Beardy who was born at Shamattawa and died in Thompson. His mother, Flora Thomas of Fort Severn, died in The Pas. His paternal grandparents were Mary and Magnus Beardy from Shamattawa; his maternal grandparents were Maggie and Thomas Thomas from Fort Severn.

Fred spent his childhood in the Kaskatamagun and York Factory areas. He did not go to school but he learned to speak English while working with the Reverend Richard Faries at York Factory. His father taught him to hunt and trap. Fred married Isabel Thomas at York Factory and has eight surviving children. His second marriage, to Sarah, the widow of Barnabas Beardy, took place on 29 November 1983. There are no children from this marriage. From Fred's own family of ten there are six surviving siblings.

Fred left York Factory in 1957 and moved to York Landing. He often travels to York Factory whether it is to go hunting or just to visit the area. He speaks about missing the place and how sorry he is that they had to leave it.

RICHARD BEARDY

Richard Franklin Beardy, a brother of Archelaus Beardy, was born at York Factory on 27 January 1915, the youngest son of Chief Abraham Beardy and Sally Beardy. Richard spent his youth at Wanatawahak, approximately six miles up-river from York Factory. At the small settlement there, Richard's father built the family home. Richard talks about how as a young boy he often ran the distance to York Factory in the winter to attend church. In the summer the family travelled by boat to the post.

Richard married Annie Saunders on 25 July 1941 in the Church of St John of York Factory. They had five children, of whom two are deceased and the rest are living in York Landing. Both Richard and Annie have passed away since the interview was conducted in May 1990.

ALBERT AND AMY HILL

Albert Hill was born on 17 December 1905 at Puskwatenak, Manitoba. He does not know when or where his father, John Hill, was born but he died at Wanatawahak. His mother was Caroline Frank, who was born at Split Lake, Manitoba, and died at Shamattawa. His maternal grandfather, Edward Frank, was also known as *Apisk* [a very large eagle]. Albert had five brothers who are all deceased.

Amy Hill was born on 12 July 1913 at York Factory to Thomas Redhead and Maggie Beardy. She does not know when and where they were born but both parents died at Shamattawa. Her

maternal grandparents were Magnus and Mary Beardy. She has one surviving sister, Eliza Hill, who lives with her and her husband.

Albert and Amy were married at York Factory by the Reverend Richard Faries, on 2 August 1926. From a family of fourteen, they have four surviving children. During their stay at York Factory, Albert was employed by the HBC in the summer and he trapped all winter. He took his family from York Factory to Shamattawa, and then in 1957 to Gillam. Hired by Canadian National Railways, he worked there until retirement. He and Amy moved to Bird where they recently celebrated their sixty-seventh wedding anniversary. Amy passed away in June of 1996.

ELIZABETH OMAN

Elizabeth Oman was born Elizabeth Jane Wastesicoot at York Factory on 21 December 1921. Her father was Absalom Wastesicoot, was born at York Factory in 1896. He died at Kaskatamagun at age 34, on 15 October 1930. Her mother was Sarah Jean Gray, who was born at York Factory in 1892 and died there at age 35, at York Factory on 6 April 1927. Her maternal grandfather was William Gray, Sr, who died at York Factory on 24 February 1927 at age 68. She does not remember her grandmothers. Her paternal grandfather was Charles Wastesicoot.

Elizabeth went to residential school in The Pas and at Elkhorn, Manitoba. She left York Factory in 1933 and did not return until 1940. Before her family left the post, Elizabeth had lost two elder brothers, whose names she does not know, and one younger brother, Luke Wastesicoot. He died at the age of one on 28 December 1928. Her other siblings are Harry Wastesicoot, formerly of Churchill, and Alice Wastesicoot who later married Alex Ouscan of Churchill.

Elizabeth married Fred Oman from Churchill in July 1947. He was born on 4 August 1914 and died on 7 December 1987. She has two surviving children, Larry Oman and Esther Oman, who are both living in Thompson. She lost a son and a daughter to pneumonia. Elizabeth makes her home in Thompson, having left Churchill in 1982.

MARY REDHEAD

Mary Redhead is a member of the Fox Lake First Nation and lives in Bird. She was born at York Factory on 20 April 1920 to David Neepin and Victoria Beardy. She does not know when or where they were born, but they both died at Port Nelson. Her paternal grandparents were Betsy and *Kihci* [Big] George Neepin. Sandy and Mary Beardy were her maternal grandparents. She lived at York Factory until she was six years old at which time she lost her mother. Her father then took her to Port Nelson to stay with relatives.

At the age of nine Mary was sent to The Pas to attend McKay Residential School. This school later burned down and all the children were then put in school at Elkhorn. Mary did not return to York Factory until she was seventeen years old. There were five children from York, including Mary, sent out to school at that time and it was the Reverend Richard Faries who travelled to Elkhorn and took them back to York Factory. Mary remembers being hospitalized for one month while in Elkhorn after receiving word about the death of her father. She was not allowed to return home for his funeral, and the loneliness and grief she experienced during this time, she says, will always stay with her.

Mary married Billy Redhead at York Factory on 2 August 1937. She has five children who are all living in Bird. She knows that all but one of her siblings are deceased. A brother moved to Ontario and she has no idea if he is still alive. Her husband died at Gillam in December 1965. Mary always loved to dance and still does so today! She also produces beautiful beadwork and sells a lot of handicrafts.

JOHN NEEPIN

John Neepin was born on 11 October 1916 at Wanatawahak. He did not go to school and was taught by his parents and elders. His parents were Moses Neepin and Arabella Beardy. Moses was born on 10 May 1886 at York Factory and Arabella was born in 1887 at Shamattawa. They are both deceased and are buried at Churchill. His paternal grandfather was George Neepin, who was originally from Fort Severn but subsequently moved to York Factory. His maternal grandparents were Robert Beardy and Margaret Monias. Robert Beardy was from Shamattawa but later settled to York Factory.

John's wife is Mary Peters who was born at Fox Lake, Manitoba, on 28 February 1925. They were married at Gillam on 2 July 1941. John comes from a family of eight and has one sister who lives in Churchill. He spent the earlier part of his life at Wanatawahak and then moved to Port Nelson. In 1942 he left there for Gillam to find employment with Canadian National Railways. During his employment with CNR he lived at Herchemer, Mile 412 on the railway, where he lived for twenty-two years. John is now retired and he and Mary reside in Thompson. They have six children in the Thompson and Winnipeg areas.

Afterword

The sights and sounds of daily life at York Factory – the shouts of men unloading the schooner, the barking of dogs, and the laughter of children playing along the riverbank – have long since disappeared. Declared a national historic site in 1936 and closed by the company in 1957, York Factory is today a lonely spot, far from any centre of population and visited only by canoeists, hunters, and the occasional adventurous visitor interested in the history of the old post.

Little of York's past glory is evident at this once-bustling site. The majestic depot building erected in the 1830s still dominates the place, but only the traces of other structures, such as an eighteenth-century stone powder-magazine, are visible in the clearings and among the scrub willows that threaten to overrun the site. The old cemetery located near Sloop Creek contains the marked and unmarked graves of hundreds of post servants and hunters. On a number of the deteriorated crosses and headstones, many surrounded by small, painted, picket enclosures which the elements have weathered a silvery gray, can be read the names once associated with the post: Gray, McPherson, Saunders, Beardy, Spence, and Gibeault. The epitaph on one reads: "In memory of William Wastasecoot, a great hunter for 60 years. He paid his last debt in 1901; he spoke the truth and was held in esteem by all the officers he worked for. This stone is placed on his grave by one of them." In recent years their descendants, members of the York Factory First Nation in York Landing, have travelled to the site to assist in the maintenance and identification of grave markers in the cemetery. A number of York Factory elders have also returned to York at various times to reflect upon their early years at the post and to reminisce about a place that is deeply embedded in their individual and collective cultural experience.

In recent decades Parks Canada has sponsored a good deal of historical and archaeological research at York Factory. Structural histories, a land-use history, and a published social history of the post covering the period between 1788 and 1870 have been augmented by extensive archaeological investigations, including the excavation of the remains of the eighteenth-century octagonal fort located under the depot building. Over 200,000 artifacts have been collected and inventoried during the course of these investigations and many of these artifacts relate to the aboriginal presence at York Factory. A management plan guides all future preservation and interpretation efforts at York Factory National Historic Site.

Though the documentary record and archaeological investigations provide useful information about life at the post in the historic period, the oral accounts gathered here sustain a more balanced reconstruction of the past, especially the more recent past. The reminiscences of the York Factory elders reveal much about the lives of the Cree people of the region: their childhood, family and community relations, material culture, work, subsistence patterns, and world view. The elders are justifiably proud of their heritage and have expressed great interest in having these stories made available to a larger audience. It is our sincere hope that this book makes a small contribution to the preservation of their heritage and will help others to understand and appreciate the remarkable lives of the York Factory people.

Notes

1 A decline in the number of Canada geese just after World War II led to the closing of the hunting season along the Mississippi flyway in 1946. Although hunting was re-opened the following year, the next two seasons were partly restricted and the management of refuges was intensified in the late 1940s. See *Canada Geese of the Hudson Bay Lowlands* (Winnipeg: Manitoba, Department of Mines and Natural Resources 1979), 18.

2 These are traditional laws. To light a fire at night is not permitted because the light attracts the geese. To hunt after dark is also forbidden. It would not be possible to find a dead or wounded bird, and a food source would thus be wasted. It is regarded as unfair to the birds to hunt them when the air is calm. A true hunter hunts when there is a wind to carry them.

3 An overpopulation of waterfowl, for instance, increases the threat of epidemics. Viral enteritis, fowl cholera, and botulism have been known to kill tens of thousands of waterfowl within a few weeks. See *Canada Geese*, 19.

4 Geese were an extremely important food source in the York Factory area. The spring and fall goose hunts were a part of the seasonal cycle there and for many generations were a major activity of the Cree hunters who were associated with the post. One of the earliest descriptions of the hunt in the York area came from the explorer and cartographer David

Thompson, who worked for the HBC in the late eighteenth century. He wrote: "The shooting of the wild Geese (or as it is called, the hunt) is of great importance to these Factories not only for present fresh meat, but also [because it] forms a supply of Provisions for a great part of the winter ... About ten of the best shots of the men of the Factory, with several Indians, are now sent to the marshes to shoot them. [Marsh Point was a key goose hunting site in the York Factory area.] For this purpose each man has always two guns, each makes what is called a Stand, this is composed of drift wood and pine branches, about three feet high, six feet in diameter, and half round in form, to shelter himself from the weather and the view of the geese; each Stand is about 120 yards from the other, or more, and forms a line on the usual passage of the geese, [which is] always near the sea shore ... each hunter has about ten mock geese, which are sticks made and painted to resemble the head and neck of the gray goose to which is added a piece of canvas for the body ... when the geese first arrive, they readily answer the call of the Hunter. The Indians imitate them so well that they would alight among the mock geese, if the shots of the hunter did not prevent them. The geese are all shot on the wing; they are too shy, and the marsh too level, to be approached. Some good shots, in the spring hunt, kill from 70 to 90 geese, but the general average is from 40 to 50 geese p^r man, as the season may be." From *David Thompson's Narrative of His Explorations in Western North America, 1784–1812*, ed. J.B. Tyrrell (Toronto: Champlain Society 1916), 34–5. Andrew Graham provided descriptions of the different species of geese found on western Hudson Bay, as well as the Cree names for these species. See *Andrew Graham's Observations on Hudson's Bay, 1767–91*, ed. Glyndwr Williams (London: Hudson's Bay Record Society 1969), 41–5. Although they generally did not arrive until the early part of May, geese were occasionally sighted in the York area in late April. See, for instance, York Factory Journal, 29 April 1938, HBCA B.239/a/195, fo. 73. Traditional goose-hunting areas near York were at Marsh Point, Sam's Creek (a short distance north of *Pâwinakâw*/Port Nelson), and in the marshy areas along the coast east of York, at the mouth of the Machichi River. The

Machichi was usually called the Fourteens River by HBC men in the eighteenth, nineteenth, and twentieth centuries.

5 The illness is due to mercury poisoning, a result of flooding from the massive hydroelectric dams on the Nelson River. For the history of hydroelectric projects in northern Manitoba and their effect upon aboriginal communities see James Waldram, *As Long as the Rivers Run: Hydroelectric Development and Native Communities in Western Canada* (Winnipeg: University of Manitoba Press 1988).

6 Prices for silver fox furs, as for most other pelts, declined dramatically after 1928. According to HBC records. "A considerable part of the blame for the [financial] losses can be attributed to the collapse of general business in 1929 and the world-wide depression that has resulted since. Prices of practically all merchandise and furs have been reduced during the past three years to only fractions of their former values." HBCA, RG 2/22/4. Fur Trade Department, Annual Report, 1930–31, p. 7. See also fig. 26, "Changing prices, 1920–45: selected Canadian wild furs," in A.J. Ray, *The Canadian Fur Trade in the Industrial Age* (Toronto: University of Toronto Press 1990), 114.

7 According to records from the late eighteenth century, large herds of caribou, probably of the Barren-Ground subspecies, travelled in the general vicinity of York Factory in their annual spring and fall migrations. Unlike most migratory animals, caribou moved southward in the spring and northward as winter approached. Coming from the northwest, the herds crossed the still-frozen Nelson and Hayes rivers around the end of March on their way to the coastal tundra of southwestern Hudson Bay. Following ancient pathways, they returned northward in the late summer, the often huge herds crossing the Hayes about twenty to sixty miles above York Factory. See Victor Lytwyn, "The Hudson Bay Lowland Cree in the Fur Trade to 1821: A Study in Historical Geography" (PHD dissertation, University of Manitoba 1993), 200–10. Lytwyn's information on caribou migration patterns, approximate herd size, and the use of "deer" hedges for hunting in the 18th and early 19th centuries

comes from a variety of sources, including *Andrew Graham's Observations; James Isham's Observations on Hudsons Bay, 1743*, ed. E.E. Rich and A.M. Johnson (Toronto: Champlain Society 1949); Nicolas Jérémie, *Twenty Years of York Factory, 1694–1714*, trans. and ed. R. Douglas and J.N. Wallace (Ottawa: Thornburn and Abbot 1926); and *Documents Relating to the Early History of Hudson Bay*, ed. J.B. Tyrrell (Ottawa: Champlain Society 1931), as well as from HBC post journals of the period. Lytwyn argues that pressure on the lowland Cree (including the Cree of the York Factory area) to provide the HBC with greater quantities of country foods after 1780 led to an increase in the exploitation of animal resources beyond sustainable harvest levels, which resulted in a significant reduction in the caribou population and the eventual out-migration from the York Factory region of many lowland or Swampy Cree people after 1800 (p. 452). A survey of the York Factory journals for the period after 1920 indicates that the caribou population in the York district was much diminished from the days when Jérémie remarked that their numbers were "almost countless" and Thompson described the approach of a herd as sounding like "distant thunder". Contrast with the York Factory Journal, 1922–1930, HBCA, B.239/a/191–3.

8 The use of fish weirs by the coastal Cree was described by Andrew Graham. Weirs consisted of wooden stakes set in a fast-moving stream to form an enclosure. These box-like structures channelled the fish along a ramp opening that, when combined with fast-moving water, prevented the fish from escaping back down the ramp. A dip net was used to scoop the catch from the weir. See Kenneth Lister, "Provisioning at Fishing Stations: Fish and the Native Occupation of the Hudson Bay Lowland," *Boreal Forest and Sub-Arctic Archaeology*, Ontario Archaeological Society, Occasional Paper no. 6 (1988), 75. In the twentieth century, York Factory was partly provisioned from a fall fishery at Fishing Island, located some five miles up-river from the post near Wanatawahak.

9 According to A.J. Ray, the production of arctic fox furs between 1920 and 1945 peaked in 1923, 1931, and again in 1943. See Ray, *Canadian Fur Trade*, 158.

10 The extension of credit on food and supplies for aboriginal
hunters was a practice almost as old as the fur trade itself.
European traders, in an attempt to assure a profitable return,
advanced a quantity of goods, including such items as guns,
powder, ball, knives, kettles, tobacco, and foodstuffs, to
Native trappers in the spring or fall. Under monopolistic
conditions the credit system worked fairly well for the HBC
but it tended to break down during the period of intense
competition between 1763 and 1821, resulting in frequent
attempts by the company to restrict credit through an
aggressive collection of debts, or through limiting advances
to only those Indians whom the it considered "good" or
reliable hunters. See A.J. Ray, *Indians in the Fur Trade; Their
Role as Hunters, Trappers and Middlemen in the Lands Southwest
of Hudson Bay, 1660–1870* (Toronto: University of Toronto
Press 1974) 137–8. In the 20th century credit, or "taking
debt," remained an important feature of the fur trade,
although periodic efforts to reduce or eliminate it were made
by the HBC. In its 1927 directive "Rules and Regulations
Governing Advances to Natives and White Customers," the
company specified that no Indian or white customer was to
receive an advance that exceeded fifty per cent of the value
of his average autumn or spring hunt. The new regulation
encountered stiff resistance among Native trappers, as well
as among a number of post managers, and was eventually
relaxed by the company. See Ray, *Canadian Fur Trade*, 211–21.
In her analysis of the use of credit in the fur trade, Toby
Morantz identifies four distinct periods of fluctuating policies and attitudes by the HBC toward debt (1700–1821,
1821–1903, 1903–26, and 1926–36), which roughly coincide
with periods of monopoly and competition. For the Cree
people of James Bay, Morantz argues, the credit system was a
natural outcome of what she calls the "ideology of reciproc-
ity," wherein such items as food were shared in expectation
of some future return. See Toby Morantz, " 'Gift-Offerings to
Their Own Importance and Superiority': Fur Trade Relations, 1700–1940," *Papers of the Nineteenth Algonquian Conference*, ed. William Cowan (Ottawa: Carleton University 1988),
137–41.

11 This explanation of prices refers to the system based on "made beaver," a standard of trade used for centuries, in which the pelts from different animals were valued against the buying power of one prime adult beaver skin. First adopted by the HBC prior to the introduction of a monetary currency, the "made beaver" standard persisted in some isolated areas of the north well into the late 19th century. At such posts as York Factory, furs, country provisions, store purchases, and even labour were listed in account books in "made beaver" or MB values as late as the 1870s. See, for instance, York Factory Indian Work Accounts, 1873–75, HBCA B.239/1277. According to these accounts one day's labour with the company at that time was worth approximately one-half MB. Four pounds of sugar was valued at two MB, or four days' labour.

12 Drag-, or seine-nets were often used by local people to catch fish when rivers and streams were free from ice, while gill-nets could be operated under the ice during the winter months. The latter technique was described by Christopher Middleton in the eighteenth century in his "Account of the Extraordinary Degrees and Surprizing effects of Cold in Hudson's Bay," reprinted in *The Voyage of Christopher Middleton, 1741–1742*, ed. William Barr and Glyndwr Williams (London: Hakluyt Society 1994), 225–6.

13 Whale-oil was used by local people for cooking and as fuel for oil-burning lamps. White, or beluga whales were caught with nets or killed with harpoons, usually near the estuaries of the Hayes and Nelson rivers. Historically, whale meat was used for dog food or was sold to the HBC. In the 18th century Graham noted that many beluga, or "Wapameg," whales were "killed annually which supply the Factories with oil, and furnish several tons to be imported to England." *Andrew Graham's Observations*, 116.

14 Coast boats were introduced by the company in the late nineteenth century and were used to transport goods between bayside posts or between the annual supply ship and the post. Measuring approximately forty-eight feet in length, coast

boats were single- or double-masted, fore-and-aft rigged, open-decked vessels that could carry from ten to fifteen tons of cargo. Notoriously difficult to handle in the rough and often windy conditions of Hudson Bay, coast boats were replaced with motorized schooners by the company early in the 20th century. For information on particular coast boats at York Factory see HBCA, B.239/a/184 and B.239/a/1484 and 1486.

15 Ciscoes, or lake herring, average from eight to twelve inches in length and are found in the lakes and rivers of the Hudson Bay region. A whitefish, ciscoes were often called "tullibees," especially by nineteenth-century fur traders. This latter term, according to Sir John Richardson (1836), came from the Cree word *ottonneebees*. See W.B. Scott and E.J. Crossmen, *Freshwater Fishes of Canada*, Fisheries Research Board of Canada, Bulletin no. 184 (Ottawa: 1973), 236–42. In his eighteenth-century catalogue of fish species from the Hudson Bay lowlands, Graham called ciscoes "shad fish." See *Andrew Graham's Observations*, 123.

16 The company store at York Factory was relocated to the southwest corner of the depot building in 1914. See York Factory Journal, 10 Oct. 1914, HBCA B.239/a/189. It remained in this location until the closing of the post in 1957.

17 Creating smoke in a pail was achieved by mixing wood chips with earth or muskeg, a concoction which when lit would smoulder for many hours. Apparently, this technique of protecting oneself against mosquitoes while travelling was unknown to eighteenth-century European traders who travelled in the York Factory area. David Thompson, for example, wrote that smoke provided little relief from mosquitoes and besides, he commented, "smoke cannot be carried about with us," *David Thompson's Narrative*, 24.

18 Archelaus Beardy (1912–89) and Richard Beardy (1915–91), were sons of Chief Abraham Beardy (1878–1950) and Sally Beardy (1872–1964).

19 According to Graham, the wolverine – the *quiquahack* or *carca-jow*, as it was known among the lowland Cree of the eighteenth century – was considered to be "extremely malicious and mischievous, and [does] more damage to the small fur trade than all the other animals conjunctly." He also noted that the wolverine was known to "follow a person's track through a gang of traps forty, fifty or even a hundred miles, and render the whole unserviceable merely to come at the baits." *Andrew Graham's Observations*, 20. Thompson described the wolverine as "by nature a plunderer, and mischievous, he is the plague of the country." *David Thompson's Narrative*, 74.

20 The Owl River drains into Hudson Bay about fifty miles north of Port Nelson.

21 Wapinayo/White Partridge Creek is located along the coast approximately twenty-five miles north of *Pâwinakâw*/Port Nelson.

22 Local men were hired by the company, usually on a daily basis, to unload and load the coast boats and schooners that regularly arrived at the factory. Such schooners as the *Fort York* and the *Fort Severn* also serviced the post regularly during this period.

23 York boats were first developed by the HBC for inland transport in the eighteenth century and were still being used in parts of northern Manitoba well into the 1920s. Varying in length from twenty-seven to forty-two feet, York boats could carry up to three and one-half tons of freight and generally had a crew of up to eight oarsmen. Boat crews were often forced to use drag lines to haul the boats through rapids or against strong currents. The boats were constructed at York until the 1840s when the bulk of this activity was shifted by the company to Norway House. See Richard Glover, "York Boats," *The Beaver* (March 1949), 19–23.

24 The depot building at York Factory, a two and one-half storey, 18,000-square-foot, wood-frame warehouse built between

1832 and 1838, served as the factory's main storage bulding for almost 120 years. Like almost all construction at the post, the depot sits on a foundation of large, squared, sill logs. The building stands today and is traditionally known as *Kihci-wâskâhikan*, or Great House among local Cree trappers. For a history of the depot building see Bruce Donaldson, *The York Factory 'Depot' Warehouse – Style and Construction*, Parks Canada, Research Bulletin no. 184 (Ottawa: February 1983).

25 Mr Hatley, with his wife Diane, has owned and operated the Silver Goose Lodge at York Factory since 1985. Prior to that Hatley was involved in operating a goose camp at Sîpâstik/Ten Shilling Creek near York Factory.

26 Dances and feasts were regularly held at York Factory, particularly during the summer months. According to the post journal these celebrations often coincided with the arrival of the supply ship or the arrival of trappers who travelled to York in springtime from their winter camps inland. After its construction in 1919 the "Indian Council House," located a short distance up-river from the factory at a small settlement area known as The Bight, was the site of many of these dances. The Bight was formerly part of the 7.7-acre Anglican Mission property and was partially abandoned by 1920 because of evictions that resulted from the transfer of land to the Anglican diocese. See York Factory Journal, HBCA B.239/a/195, fo. 2, fo. 4.

27 Possibly the *Erik*, a three-masted, ship-rigged, screw steamer that serviced HBC posts in the Hudson Bay, James Bay, and Ungava districts between 1892 and 1901, or possibly the *Pelican*, a smaller screw sloop that supplied York Factory until 1916.

28 George R. Ray served as post manager at York Factory between 1906 and 1908 and as head of the HBC's Nelson River District between 1911 and 1914. Shortly after, Ray left the company and in 1916, along with his son, established an independent post at "Wannatocca, on the banks of the Hayes River,

about 10 miles south of York Factory." A.W. Patterson to Fur
Trade Commissioner, 2 September 1916, HBCA, D.FTR/5,
fo. 45. In 1917 Ray moved his operation closer to York and
established a store at Wanatawahak/Crooked Bank. An effec-
tive trader, Ray secured with his son the contract to supply the
Royal North-West Mounted Police detachment at *Pâwinakâw/*
Port Nelson in 1918 and soon captured more than fifty per
cent of the York Factory, Shamattawa, and Trout Lake fur
trade. The HBC responded to Ray's competition in typical
fashion and purchased his operation in 1920. See York Factory
Journal, 8 July 1920, HBCA, B.239/a/190.

29 The Mistikokan River flows into Hudson Bay just west of
   Cape Tatnum and about twenty-five miles east of York
   Factory.

30 Sam Saunders is frequently mentioned in the York Factory
   post journal between 1917 and 1920 as an "Indian trader."
   He later worked as a servant at the post and as a crew member aboard the *Mooswa*. See York Factory Journal, HBCA,
   B.239/a/189 and 190.

31 Charley Rabiska or Rabiscah. See York Factory Journal,
   1903–1904, HBCA B.239/a/185.

32 The thirty-ton steam tug *Mooswa* was sent to York Factory
   in 1910. See York Factory Journal, 6 September 1910, HBCA
   B.239/a/186. Too light to handle the rough waters of Hudson
   Bay, the *Mooswa* was wrecked in 1916 in a fall storm on the
   coast between Kaskatamagun and the Mistikokan River. See
   York Factory Journal, 28 September 1916, HBCA, B.239/a/189,
   fo. 189.

33 The Hayes River generally begins to break up around the end
   of May. See, for instance, York Factory Journal, 1 June 1937,
   HBCA B.239/a/195, fo. 1.

34 Mr Hill is describing an area approximately sixteen by twenty
   feet.

35 Mr Beardy may be referring to coast boats or flat-bottomed scows, or perhaps to York boats, which could be equipped with sails when the need arose.

36 See note 10.

37 *Kihci-pôcôw* is a derogatory term for a person for whom the local people had little or no respect. See Abel Chapman's comments above.

38 "Big boss" refers here to the post manager. Local Cree people sometimes referred to the company clerks, or other whites at York, as "boss," although the designation "big boss" was usually reserved for the post manager.

39 Chief Abraham Beardy, 1878–1950.

40 The reference here is to the "made beaver" system of value. See note 11.

41 *Paskwastikwân* translates as "bald head" and here refers to a bald or balding independent trader who, for a brief time in the 1930s, operated at *Sîpâstik*/Ten Shilling Creek.

42 Trader George R. Ray. See note 28.

43 Independent trader Luke Clemons who operated in the York region from a home base at Kettle Rapids on the Nelson River. Clemons also outfitted other independent traders in the area.

44 Chief Abraham Beardy, the chief of the York Factory band for over forty years.

45 See note 51.

46 "Football" here refers to what North Americans now commonly call soccer. This sport had a long tradition on the west coast of Hudson Bay, being mentioned as early as 1734 at Prince of Wales' Fort at Churchill (although the "rules" of the

eighteenth-century game bore little resemblance to those of
the modern sport). At York Factory, football was not mentioned until 1776 when it became a regular activity at the post
during the Christmas season. For a discussion of football as a
leisure activity at York Factory in the eighteenth and nineteenth centuries see Michael Payne, *The Most Respectable Place
in the Territory: Everyday Life in Hudson's Bay Company Service,
York Factory, 1788 to 1870*, National Historic Parks and Sites,
Studies in Archaeology, Architecture and History (Ottawa:
1989), 67–8.

47 Although an open field in the area of the Anglican Mission
property was apparently used for football (soccer) matches in
the 1920s and 1930s, a playing-field, complete with goalposts,
also existed just up-river from the depot building. See the
1930 plan of York Factory, pp. xxx and xxxi.

48 "Kissing Day" for Cree people refers to the old fur trade tradition of visiting house to house on New Year's Day, drinking
tea and brandy and exchanging kisses and handshakes. This
tradition was apparently widespread in the fur trade and was
also a customary part of the holiday season in nineteenth-
century Red River. See M.A. McLeod, "Red River New Year,"
The Beaver (December 1953), 43–7.

49 Probably Chris Harding, York Factory post manager and Nelson River District manager between 1919 and 1931.

50 That is, the bridesmaids and their partners.

51 Multiple weddings were fairly common at York Factory in this
period. See, for instance, the photograph on p. 34.

52 The Reverend Richard Faries built his parsonage in 1915 at the
Anglican Church property some distance upstream from
the post proper. As the new church at the mission property
was not constructed until 1934, summer weddings before that
date were held at the Church of St John of York Factory which
was built in 1858 near Sloop Creek and torn down in 1934.

53 A large number of edible berries grow in the Hudson Bay
lowlands. These include cranberries, strawberries, rasp-
berries or yellow-berries, gooseberries, crowberries or maw-
sberries, willowberries, partridge berries, dewberries,
huckleberries, juniper berries, black currants, red currants
and white currants. These varieties are also mentioned in
Andrew Graham's Observations, 132. Berries were a traditional
source of subsistence when other resources were scarce
and were often dried and stored for later consumption. Traditionally, they were used to flavour dried meat and fish, as
well as other foods. See Lytwyn, "Hudson Bay Lowland
Cree," 243.

54 Willow ptarmigan, known as *Wâpinêw* to the lowland Cree
and "partridges" to the men of the coastal factories, were historically an important food source for the people of the York
Factory area. Ptarmigan were generally hunted in winter,
sometimes with nets but most often with guns and birdshot.
In good years these birds were taken by the thousands and
formed a staple part of the diet of the people, both aboriginal
and non-aboriginal, who lived at York Factory.

55 Historically, polar bears were hunted for food and rendered
fat in the fall, prior to their migration north to the Cape
Churchill area. By the twentieth century, however, as other
food sources became available to the people of the York Factory area, polar bear meat became less desirable as a dietary
supplement.

56 See note 13.

57 *Wanatoyak,* or burls, are dense, knot-like growths found on the
white birch tree.

58 This method of constructing a birchbark canoe was a traditional one and remained basically unchanged from the
method employed by the Cree of Hudson Bay in the late
eighteenth century as described by Andrew Graham. See
Andrew Graham's Observations, 189–91.

59 The use of caribou hides as a tent covering in the eighteenth century is described by Graham: "The tent-cloth is made of elk or deerskin dressed, chiefly the former; from eight to twelve of which is the usual complement ... when it is put round it is tied by strings." Ibid., 185.

60 Eliza Beardy, a widow from Island Lake who raised Catherine after the death of her parents.

61 This method of processing hides was described by Graham: "[The hide] is then put into warm water and rubbed over with the brains or liver of animals; it is then stretched by lacing it to a strong willow tied in a circular form. When dry it is hung up to smoke in the tent, then scraped again to take off the Thorny filaments; and nothing more remains to be done but rubbing it well to make it perfectly soft, which is performed by pulling it backwards and forwards over a string." See *Andrew Graham's Observations*, 188. See also June Helm, "Women's Work, Women's Art," in Barbara Hail and Kate Duncan, *Out of the North: The Subarctic Collection of the Haffenreffer Museum of Anthropology* (Bristol, RI: Haffenreffer Museum of Anthropology 1989), 121.

62 Billy Redhead, Mary's husband, whom she married in 1937.

63 A similar method was described by Graham in the eighteenth century: "They have a kind of bag made of cloth, or leather, in which the child is laced after being laid perfectly straight, with the hands along the sides. In the day time, or when travelling, this is put into the back-board or cradle." See *Andrew Graham's Observations*, 178.

64 Eliza Oman, who worked as a cook for the HBC at York Factory in the 1920s and 1930s. See photograph p. 29.

65 Out of respect for those who have passed away, people do not mention their name when referring to them. Abel Chapman later mentioned his daughter's name but when he first started telling the story he referred to it as "The Birth" or "Being

Born" on this date and month. Many elders use these terms
when speaking of a loved one who has passed on.

66 Referring to Christianity.

67 Hudson Bay.

68 The Cree word *êmistikôsiw* translates as "white man," while
the term *êmistikôsimowin* refers to "English," the language of
these white men. As religious services were held in English in
this particular church at York Factory, it was referred to as the
"English" church.

69 The "English" church was also called locally the "iron" or
"tin" church. Made of corrugated iron and erected in 1873
under the direction of the Reverend William Kirkby of the
Church Missionary Society, this prefabricated building, which
could seat up to 100 people, was originally intended for the
mission at Churchill but was considered too large for that
location. Measuring eighteen by thirty-six feet, the "tin"
church was put up just behind, and slightly downstream
from, the depot building near the old tradesmen's shops. See
Bruce Donaldson, "York Factory: A Land-Use History" (Parks
Canada, Manuscript Report Series no. 444, 1981), 91–2.

70 The Church of St John of York Factory, referred to historically
as simply the "Indian" or "Cree" church, was designed by
Chief Factor James Hargrave and was constructed in 1858.
Located down-river from the post near Sloop Creek, the
church measured fifty by twenty-five feet and had a spire
sixty-six feet in height. The building was torn down in 1934.
See Donaldson, "York Factory: A Land-Use History," 64–5.

71 Located at the Anglican Mission property up-river from the
factory, this church (also called St John of York Factory)
was constructed in 1934 to replace the 1858 building. It was
demolished in the early 1970s. Stained-glass windows, pews,
and a baptismal font from the church were moved at that time
onto the second floor of the depot building by caretaker

Douglas MacLachlan. The Lady Franklin window, given by
the widow of the arctic explorer Sir John Franklin as a memo-
rial to her husband and in recognition of those who took part
in the search for the missing expedition, was originally in-
stalled in the 1858 church and later moved to the 1934 building. It was eventually sent to Churchill where it currently
graces St Paul's Anglican Church in that community.

72 Faries, an Anglican priest, arrived at York Factory in 1899 and
retired from the post in 1950, having served an incredible
fifty-one years as the resident minister. Faries's journal, which
covers the years between 1899 and 1937, is in the Diocese of
Keewatin Office of the Anglican Church of Canada, in Kenora,
Ontario. The first permanent missionary at York Factory was
the Reverend William Mason of the Church Missionary
Society who came to the post in 1854. His successors, prior
to Faries's arrival, included Joseph Gardiner and William
Kirkby. See Payne, *Most Respectable Place in the Territory,*
114–18.

73 The "iron" or "tin" church.

74 After Faries retired from York Factory in 1950 the Anglican
Church abandoned the post as a permanent mission site and
church services for the community were carried on by George
Saunders, a local Native lay preacher, until the closing of
the post in 1957. During this period the bishop of Keewatin
also made occasional fly-in visits to the community in order
to perform weddings and baptisms. See York Factory Baptismal Register, 1932–1957, Anglican Church of Canada, Diocese
of Keewatin Office, as well as Donaldson, "York Factory:
A Land-Use History," 116.

75 A school of one sort or another had existed at York Factory
since relatively early in the post's history. The first attempt at
providing a semblance of formal education at York actually
dates to 1807 with the appointment by the HBC of William
Garrioch as local schoolmaster. The school was designed for
the children of post servants in order to provide the company

with, in the words of the London Committee, "a Colony of
very useful hands." The post school operated only intermit-
tently, however, until the arrival of the Reverend William
Mason in 1854 when it was expanded and formalized. See
Payne, *The Most Respectable Place in the Territory*, 107–13 and
Jennifer S.H. Brown " 'A Colony of Very Useful Hands,' " *The
Beaver* (Spring 1977), 39–45. In 1863 the Church Missionary
Society sent a prefabricated school building to York which
was erected just downstream from the "iron" church. In 1880
a new log school was constructed nearby, even though the
local school population had declined by that time because
York's importance as a trading centre had diminished and
many Native families had begun moving away. In 1912, with
the expansion of the Manitoba boundary northward, the HBC
received a grant from the provincial Department of Education
for the construction of a new school at York and a teacher
arrived that same year. Native education at York remained
under the control of the Anglican Church, however, and
Mr Faries received an annual grant of $500 from the federal
Department of Indian Affairs to operate the "Indian School"
at the post. This school, which served the children of the
handful of Cree families living nearby, was open chiefly in the
summer months when local families came off the trapline. In
1937 a new schoolhouse was constructed on the upstream side
of the depot building. Later converted to a residence for the
site caretaker, it burned to the ground in the fall of 1979.
Department of Indian Affairs records indicate an average of
thirty-two pupils at the York Factory school between 1920 and
1939. See Donaldson, "York Factory: A Land-Use History,"
108, 115, 118, 186. At the same time many local Cree children
were also sent to residential schools as part of a government
attempt to assimilate Native children into white culture. The
negative impact of these schools on aboriginal children is
only now beginning to be understood and addressed. See the
accounts of life at a residential school below.

76 Practical jokes were an everyday part of life in a community
like York Factory and often a large number of people were
involved. In this particular case the joke was on the local

children, fooling them into believing that they were to have
new schoolteachers.

77 McKay Residential School in The Pas was founded in 1918
and burned down fifteen years later in 1933.

78 Elkhorn Residential School originally known as the Washa-
kāda Indian Home, opened in June of 1888 with eight students. Closed in May of 1918, the Elkhorn school reopened in
January of 1924 as the Anglican Indian Residential School.
It closed permanently in June 1949.

79 Peter Massan's daughter.

80 David Massan may be referring to the outbreak of scarlet fever that occurred in the mid-1920s in the York-Severn region.
In the winter and spring of 1925 the post journal reported a
number of deaths at York and the immediate area, although
the journal entries do not specifically state scarlet fever, but
rather to an "epidemic of measles" at the post. See York Factory Journal, 18 January 1925, HBCA B.239/a/191, fo. 86. As
there is some similarity in symptoms between the two illnesses (such as a rash) the post manager was possibly con-
fused as to the exact nature of the infection. See Fred Beardy's
comments regarding scarlet fever below.

81 This might be a reference to the Crane Indians (or *Ocicâhko-
sak*), a northern Algonquian Oji-Cree group of the Sandy,
Big Trout, and Weagamow Lakes area, south of Fort Severn in
northern Ontario. See Edward S. Rogers and Mary Black
Rogers, "Who Were the Cranes? Groups and Group Identity
Names in Northern Ontario," *Approaches to Algonquian Archaeology: Proceedings of the Thirteenth Annual Conference*, ed. M.G.
Hanna and B. Kooyman (Calgary: University of Calgary
Archaeological Association 1982) 147–88. Rogers and Rogers
trace the group name Crane Indians to approximately 1800
and an individual named Crane (*Ocicâhk*) and his numerous
sons and sons-in-law whose territory in interior northern
Ontario was remote from early trade routes. The inhabitants

of this area, the authors argue, were virtually unknown to European traders prior to the time of Crane in the late eighteenth century.

82 A Dr Larose also visited York Factory in the 1920s. See York Factory Journal, 15 July 1925, HBCA, B.239/a/192, fo. 5.

83 Tom Lamb, the son of T.H.P. Lamb, an independent trader at Moose Lake, east of The Pas, founded Lamb's Air Service in 1935. Headquartered at The Pas and operated by the Lamb family for two generations, Lamb's Air Service flew to much of northern Manitoba. See Sydney Augustus Keighley, *Trader, Tripper, Trapper: The Life of a Bay Man* (Winnipeg: Rupert's Land Research Centre and Watson and Dwyer Publishing 1989), 22.

84 *Kâkikêpakwa*, or Labrador tea (*Ledum groenlandicum*), was known to eighteenth-century European traders as *wishekapacwaw* and was traditionally used as a plaster to treat sores and skin problems, or brewed as a tea to treat nervous disorders and rheumatic complaints. See *Andrew Graham's Observations*, 130. See also Isham's description of the medicinal properties of Labrador tea in *James Isham's Observations*, 134. He wrote, "I was troubled very much myself with a Nervous Disorder, but by Constant Drinking [of Labrador tea] 1 pint made strong for three months Entirely cur'd me."

85 Reports of the influenza epidemic in the region appeared regularly in the York Factory post journal throughout the winter, spring and summer of 1927. District manager Harding reported in February that "the present flu epidemic is of a very vicious nature" York Factory Journal, 26 February 1927, (HBCA, B.239/a/192, fo. 57) and the deaths of a number of children and older people were recorded over the next six or seven months.

86 As more modern, repeat-action rifles were expensive and sometimes hard to come by, the use of older flintlock guns persisted in the York area as late as the early twentieth century.

87 The influenza epidemic mentioned above.

88 Mrs Eli Spence.

89 *Wîhkês* is the sweet flag (*Acornus calamus*).

90 A doctor or surgeon was present at York Factory throughout
much of its history and local families were sometimes
brought to the post for medical treatment. According to
Michael Payne the HBC provided surgeons at its major bayside factories throughout the eighteenth century, and
although for the most part this practice continued over the
next two centuries, the post surgeon often served, at least
part time, in some other function, such as a clerk or writer.
Thomas Bunn, for instance, who was stationed at York in
the early part of the nineteenth century, served as the post
doctor but was listed in the records as a writer in personnel
records. As Payne notes, surgeons occupied a somewhat
ambiguous position in the post community. Although ac-
corded the status of officers and paid accordingly, post surgeons seemed to have little influence on the affairs of the
factory and often spent only a few years in the company's
service. Their medical skills varied, and while some like
Thomas Hutchins and William Todd appear from the records
to be highly skilled, others, according to Payne, "took a
rather cavalier approach to their responsibilities." See Michael
Payne, "Daily Life on Western Hudson Bay, 1714 to 1870:
A Social History of York Factory and Churchill" (PHD dissertation, Carleton University 1989), 315–17. In the twentieth
century the factory usually had a company officer who
possessed some medical knowledge, or at least had access to
a good medical text, while doctors who regularly travelled
to remote northern communities made periodic visits to
York, especially during the outbreaks of scarlet fever and
influenza.

91 The word describing a person in this state of mind is *mahîhkan*
which means "wolf," referring to "crazy as a wolf" or "crazed
wolf."

92 Before the arrival of Christianity, if people had terribly
   bad luck or got sick for no reason, it was believed that a curse
   had been put on them. Shamans, sorcerers, and medicine
   men were thought to have that power. Not all used their
   powers towards evil or harm but jealousy, anger, or envy can
   bring on such actions. Because in this account the man
   and his wife were blessed with twin girls, he believed that he
   was made ill, cursed by a person who was envious of him.
   Someone was angered because he had too much (referring
   to the twins). So the father believed that one twin had to be
   sacrificed in order for him to get well. It's sad but I [Flora
   Beardy] have often heard of this conviction. If a person
   with any healing powers used his or her power for harming
   others, the understanding is that the family in a future
   generation will pay for those actions. In my case, when the
   healing power was passed down to me, the emphasis was on
   healing and not harming. Mr and Mrs Hill and I discussed
   this issue and they both agreed that it be recorded and
   published.

93 A dry dock was constructed by the HBC at York Factory in
   1915 to provide a safe wintering berth for the schooners and
   coast boats that serviced the post. Previously, the company's
   larger vessels had been wintered at Marsh Point or at Sloop
   Creek, but these arrangements had proved less than satisfac-
   tory since the boats often suffered damage from winter ice
   and were difficult to refloat come springtime. The dry dock
   was constructed just downstream from Sloop Creek near the
   cemetery, and extended some 32 yards back from the river's
   edge. In the fall, prior to freeze-up, the boats were winched
   along wooden rails that extended approximately half the
   length of the slip. Two large anchors, partially buried in the
   ground (and still visible today), were used to secure the
   winching cables. See York Factory Journal, 30 September 1915,
   7 October 1915, HBCA, B.239/a/189.

94 Ditches were used by the company at York Factory to drain
   surface water from the post's wet, marshy ground to the river.
   The major drainage ditches that once surrounded the factory

palisade were fed by numerous smaller drains within the
post itself. Many of these drains were lined with wooden
casings and were covered in the fall to prevent their
filling with snow and debris during the winter. See Donaldson, "York Factory: A Land-Use History," 66–7. Today,
the sides of these drains have slumped dramatically and
in a few locations have eroded so badly that small ramps
have been constructed to facilitate movement across
them.

95 A "dog meat house" or "blubber house" was constructed in
the late nineteenth century and was located near the riverbank, upstream from the depot building. This building was
demolished sometime in the 1940s.

96 Mr Beardy may be referring here to government repre-
sentatives who perhaps wore some type of pilot's uniform
similar to the jackets given to the local chiefs at treaty
time.

97 At the mission property, approximately one-half mile from
the post.

98 Hay Island.

99 McLintock, on the Hudson Bay Railway, approximately
half-way between York Factory and Churchill.

100 *Cahkokâp* translates as "short person," or "Shorty."

101 Two field pieces, situated near the river in front of the depot
building, were used to signal the arrival of the supply ship
at the factory. These guns were left at the post by the British
Sixth Regiment of Foot, the Royal Warwickshires, as it
travelled through York on its way to Red River in 1846. Evi-
dently, they proved too cumbersome to freight on the York
boats that conveyed the troops to the settlement. They
are now part of the curatorial collection of Parks Canada,
Prairie Region.

102 *Mîsîwikitik* translates as "dirty knees," a joking nickname given to Robert Beardy because of his ten wives.

103 The HBC.

104 *Wîsahkêcâhk* is a mythical character in Cree legends who is usually a creator or trickster. In this story he takes on the role of the trickster. For discussion of *Wîsahkêcâhk* and his role in Cree cosmology see Jennifer Brown and Robert Brightman, *"The Orders of the Dreamed," George Nelson on Cree and Northern Ojibwa Religion and Myth, 1823* (Winnipeg: University of Manitoba Press 1988) 108, 125–36. See also Robert Brightman *Acaoohkiwina and Acimowina: Traditional Narratives of the Rock Cree Indians*, Canadian Ethnology Service, Mercury Series Paper no.113 (Ottawa: Canadian Museum of Civilization 1989), 61–6.

105 For information on the role of *Kayânwî, Wêmisôs,* and *Cahkâpês* in Cree mythology see Brightman, *Acaoohkiwina*, 73–4, 131–3, 140–2.

106 An organ exists inside the moose that contains the tracks of a frog!

107 Although furs were still brought to York Factory for trade in this period, usually in the spring, company employees were often sent inland during the winter months to trade for furs at the camps of various trappers. These "trippers" or "camp traders," as they were sometimes called, secured furs that might otherwise have gone to the independent traders who operated in the Nelson River District. Dog team was the usual mode of travel and according to the post journal these journeys lasted anywhere from two days to two weeks. See, for example, York Factory Journal, 4 April, 7 April 1922, HBCA B.239/a/191, fo. 8.

108 The Pennycutaway River flows into the Hayes approximately twenty-five miles upstream from York Factory.

109 Independent trader George R. Ray. See note 28.

110 Mr Saunders could be referring to the movement of a number
     of York families to the Shamattawa area after the company's
     re-establishment of a trading outpost there in 1904.

111 "The time of money," or *kâ-sôniyâskak*, was a phrase com-
     monly used by the people of York Factory to refer to treaty
     day at the post and the handing out of supplies and cash
     annuities to band members, usually in July each year. The
     Cree of York Factory gained treaty status in 1910 with the
     signing of an adhesion to Treaty Five. Treaty Five originated
     in two historical processes. The southern part of the treaty,
     negotiated in 1875, covered part of Manitoba's interlake
     district, the lower Saskatchewan River, and the shield coun-
     try east of Lake Winnipeg. Aboriginal people living north of
     this geographical area were not included in the original
     1875 treaty and over the next thirty years bands from Nor-
     way House, Oxford House, Island Lake, Split Lake, Nelson
     River, Deer's Lake, Churchill, and York Factory petitioned
     the federal government for adhesions to the treaty. The
     northern part of Treaty Five, negotiated in 1908–10, included
     lands located north of the 1875 treaty boundary. In 1908 the
     band at York Factory officially requested treaty and two
     years later, on 10 August 1910, York Factory chief Charles
     Wastasecoot concluded an agreement with treaty commis-
     sioner John Semmens. Well aware of the changing economy
     of northern Manitoba after 1900, the York Factory band
     negotiated the "extinguishment" of their aboriginal title to
     the area in return for reserve lands, access to subsistence
     resources, certain provisions such as ammunition, and a gra-
     tuity amounting to five dollars per person, per year. For a
     discussion of Treaty Five, including its origins, terms, and
     economic consequences see Kenneth Coates and William
     Morrison, *Treaty Five* (Ottawa: Department of Indian and
     Northern Affairs, Treaties and Historical Research Centre
     1986) and Frank Tough, "Economic Aspects of Aboriginal
     Title in Northern Manitoba: Treaty 5 Adhesions and Métis
     Scrip," *Manitoba History* 15 (Spring 1988): 3–16. For the text

of Treaty Five see Alexander Morris, *The Treaties of Canada with the Indians of Manitoba and the North-West Territories*, (1880; reprint, Toronto: Coles Publishing 1979).

112 The scarlet fever and influenza epidemics of the 1920s.

113 Royal Canadian Mounted Police. A detachment was located at nearby Pâwinakâw/Port Nelson until 1934 when it was transferred to Gillam. A detachment of the Royal North-West Mounted Police (as they were then known), comprising a sergeant and a constable, was located at York Factory for one year in 1912–13. See the letter from F.J.A. Demers, RNWMP superintendent at Churchill, to the commissioner in Regina, 13 September 1913 in National Archives of Canada, RG 18, RCMP, vol. 450, file 584–13.

114 Indicating a size approximately one by one-and-a-half feet.

115 HBC point blankets.

116 *Mahîhkan* translates as "wolf"; see also p. 66 and note 91.

117 *Tihkinâkans* means cradle boards.

118 After almost three centuries of operation York Factory was closed by the HBC in June 1957. With the company's decision to transfer its headquarters for the Nelson River District from York to Churchill in 1929 and to Winnipeg in 1931, the volume of business at the post had declined. In 1933 York lost its status as a federal customs port of entry and the next year the RCMP detachment at nearby Port Nelson was transferred to Gillam. A number of local families left York Factory in the 1930s, bound for Split Lake, Shamattawa, and new communities that were springing up along the railway. With revenues from the post totalling only $34,000 in 1956–57, the company decided to abandon it. See Malvina Bolus, "The End Comes," *The Beaver* (Winter, 1957), 56–9. In 1936 York Factory was declared a national historic site by the Historic Sites and Monuments Board of Canada, primarily for its role

in the French-English struggle for control of Hudson Bay, and in 1959 a plaque was erected at the site. In 1968 ownership of the property was officially transferred from the HBC to the federal government.

119 The new communities at Gillam and York Landing. York Landing was established in 1957 upon the closing of York Factory. Its site was chosen by the Department of Indian Affairs; local people were unfamiliar with the area. Gillam was also chosen for resettlement, primarily because of the availability of jobs on the railway.

120 A.B. McIvor (perhaps nicknamed Joe), the last post manager at York Factory.

Suggestions for Further Reading

Ahenakew, Freda, and H.C. Wolfart, eds. 1992. *Our Grandmothers' Lives as Told in Their Own Words*. Saskatoon: Fifth House Publishers.

Brightman, Robert A. 1989. *Acaoohkiwina and Acimowina: Traditional Narratives of the Rock Cree Indians*. Canadian Ethnology Service, Mercury Series Paper no. 113. Ottawa: Canadian Museum of Civilization.

– 1993. *Grateful Prey: Rock Cree Human-Animal Relationships*. Berkeley: University of California Press.

Brown, Jennifer S.H. 1986. "Northern Algonquians from Lake Superior and Hudson Bay to Manitoba in the Historical Period." In *Native Peoples: The Canadian Experience*, edited by R. Bruce Morrison and C. Roderick Wilson. Toronto: McClelland and Stewart.

– and Robert Brightman. 1988. *"The Orders of the Dreamed," George Nelson on Cree and Northern Ojibwa Religion and Myth, 1823*. Winnipeg: University of Manitoba Press.

Cruikshank, Julie (with Angela Sidney, Kitty Smith, and Annie Ned). 1990. *Life Lived Like A Story: Life Stories of Three Yukon Native Elders*. Vancouver: University of British Columbia Press.

Flannery, Regina. 1995. *Ellen Smallboy: Glimpses of a Cree Woman's Life*. Montreal and Kingston: McGill-Queen's University Press.

Honigmann, John J. 1981. "West Main Cree." In *Handbook of North American Indians*, Vol. 6, *Subarctic*, edited by June Helm, 217–30. Washington: Smithsonian Institution.

Keighley, Sydney Augustus (in collaboration with Renée Fossett Jones and David Riddle). 1989. *Trader, Tripper, Trapper: The Life of a Bay Man*. Winnipeg: Rupert's Land Research Centre and Watson and Dwyer Publishing.

Lytwyn, Victor P. 1993. "The Hudson Bay Lowland Cree in the Fur Trade to 1821: A Study in Historical Geography." PHD dissertation, University of Manitoba.

Payne, Michael. 1989. *The Most Respectable Place in the Territory: Everyday Life in Hudson's Bay Company Service, York Factory, 1788 to 1870*. Studies in Archaeology, Architecture and History. Ottawa: National Historic Parks and Sites.

– 1989. "Daily Life on Western Hudson Bay, 1714 to 1870: A Social History of York Factory and Churchill." PHD dissertation, Carleton University.

Pentland, David H. 1981. "Synonymy." In John J. Honigmann "West Main Cree." In *Handbook of North American Indians*, Vol. 6, *Subarctic*, edited by June Helm, 227–8. Washington: Smithsonian Institution.

Ray, Arthur J. 1974. *Indians in the Fur Trade; Their Role as Hunters, Trappers and Middlemen in the Lands Southwest of Hudson Bay, 1660–1870*. Toronto: University of Toronto Press.

– 1982. "York Factory: The Crisis of Transition, 1870–80." *The Beaver* 313(2): 26–31.

– 1990. *The Canadian Fur Trade in the Industrial Age*. Toronto: University of Toronto Press.

Rich, E.E., and A.M. Johnson, eds. 1949. *James Isham's Observations on Hudsons Bay, 1743*. Toronto: Champlain Society.

Tough, Frank. 1988. "Economic Aspects of Aboriginal Title in Northern Manitoba: Treaty 5 Adhesions and Métis Scrip." *Manitoba History* 15: 3–16.

– 1996. *'As Their Natural Resources Fail': Native Peoples and the Economic History of Northern Manitoba, 1870–1930*. Vancouver: UBC Press.

Williams, Glyndwr, ed. 1969. *Andrew Graham's Observations on Hudson's Bay, 1767–91*. London: Hudson's Bay Record Society.

Index

bowling (game), 51
buildings at York Factory, Cree:
Indian Council House, 131;
HBC: depot, 130–1; dog meat
house, 67, 144; dry dock, 66,
143; store, 129; missions: parsonage, 39, 134. *See also under*
churches
bull, Richard Faries's, 58, 73
Bunn, Thomas, 142

calendar, Cree origin story of,
78–9
Canada (Dominion) Day celebrations, 33–5
candies at ship time, 23, 71
cannons fired at ship time, 71–2,
144
canoe, construction of birchbark,
41–2, 135
caribou, 9, 17; decline in numbers of, 126; in diet, 40, 42; migration patterns of, 40, 125–6;
uses for, 44, 136
caribou, legendary. *See* Atik
celebrations: Canada (Dominion) Day, 33–5; Christmas,
35–7; New Year's, 37, 134;
sports days, 35; Treaty Day,
84–9
Chambers, Joe, 31
Chapman, Abel, 74–5; avoids
naming the dead, 136–7;
biography of, 105; dream of,
17; reminiscences of, 15–17,
20–1, 26, 31–3, 43–4, 47–9,
51, 57, 65, 89, 91, 92–3; traditional stories told by, 76–9;
views on human and divine
law, 57
children, care of, 11, 47, 90, 136;
play of, 44, 51; toys for, 43, 49,

51; on Treaty Day, 89; work of,
44
Christmas celebrations, 35–7, 82
Church Missionary Society,
sends prefabricated school, 139
churches at York Factory, 53–5,
134, 137–8
cigarettes, price of, 18
ciscoes (lake herring), 13–15, 129
Clemons, Luke, 33, 133
clothing, 43, 82; rabbit skin, 11, 82
commercial activities. *See under*
economic activities
conservation, Cree views on, 3, 7
cradle boards, 11, 47, 90, 136
Cranes, identification of, 140–1
Cree church. *See* St John of York
Factory
Cree (language), xvii
Cree (people), cultural change
among, xxiii, xxv, xxxvi, 75–6;
group names for, xvii; numbers at York Factory, xxiii,
xx–vii; population move-
ments among, xxv, xxvii, 57–8,
79–80, 82, 83, 91–3, 146, 147:
seasonal, xxix, 11–13, 16–17,
82; in York Factory region,
xvi–xvii, xxi–xxiii
Crooked Bank (Wanatawahak),
23, 132
Cruikshank, Julie, on autobiography, xxxii; on oral accounts,
xiv

dances and dancing, 21, 35, 131;
on Treaty Day, 84–9
death in former times, 90
diapers, moss, 47
diet, 83; bears in, 135; beaver in,
4, 8; berries in, 39, 135; caribou
in, 40, 42; fat in, 39, 40; fish in,

Todd, William, 142
toys. *See under* children
trapping, commercial, 4: outfits
    for, 10, 26, 127; methods of, 9;
    owls, 8
travel, food supply for, 15, 24–6,
    42; hunger during, 69–70;
    methods of, 11–13, 26, 79; by
    river raft, 24
Treaty Day, 84–9
Treaty Five, xxvii, 146–7
tripping (camp trade), 145
Trout River epidemic, 61
twins, sacrifice of one, 66

vaccination, xxiv

wage labour. *See under* economic
    activities
Wanatawahak, 80; summer pop-
    ulation at, 82; *see also* Crooked
    Bank
wanatoyak (white-birch burls),
    135; for domestic fire starter, 41
Wannatocca post, 131–2
wapameg. *See* whales
Wapinayo Sîpiy (White Partridge
    Creek), 17, 130
Wâpistânihk (Place of Martens),
    72
Washakada Indian Home. *See*
    Elkhorn Residential School
Wastasecoot, Charles, signs
    Treaty Five adhesion, 146
Wastasecoot, William, epitaph, 121

Wastesecoot, Solomon, 67
weddings, 33, 134
whales, in diet, 13, 40; uses for,
    11, 13, 40, 128
whaling methods, 11, 128
White Partridge Creek. *See* Wapi-
    nayo Sîpiy
widows, 79
wigwams, 43, 44, 80–2; on river
    rafts, 24
wîhkês (sweet flag), 65
Wîsahkêcâhk, 76–8, 145
wolverine, habits of, 16, 130
women, 18–20; clothing of, 43;
    correct behaviour of, 46–7;
    hunting skills of, 44, 46; trap-
    ping skills of, 8, 15, 82; wid-
    owed, 79; work of, 11, 13, 44,
    47, 49, 72
woodcutting, 31

York boats. *See under* boats
York Factory, Cree population at,
    xxiii; declared national historic
    site, 121, 147–8; as HBC supply
    centre, xx–xxi; historical
    sources on, xv; history of, xvii–
    xxi, 147–8; processing furs at,
    15; volume of trade at (1730s),
    xx
York Factory Oral History Project,
    xi–xii, xiii, xvi, xxxiii–xxxv
York Landing, xxi, 92, 148
Yule, Dr, 61